Magento 2 Theme Design

Second Edition

Create stunning and responsive Magento 2 themes for your business

Fernando J Miguel
Richard Carter

BIRMINGHAM - MUMBAI

Magento 2 Theme Design

Second Edition

Copyright © 2016 Packt Publishing

First published: July 2009

Second edition: October 2016

Production reference: 1241016

Published by Packt Publishing Ltd.
Livery Place
35 Livery Street
Birmingham
B3 2PB, UK.
ISBN 978-1-78588-822-9

www.packtpub.com

Credits

Authors

Fernando J Miguel
Richard Carter

Commissioning Editor

Wilson D'souza

Acquisition Editor

Smeet Thakkar

Content Development Editor

Parshva Sheth

Technical Editor

Rutuja Vaze

Copy Editor

Safis Editing

Project Coordinator

Ritika Manoj

Proofreader

Safis Editing

Indexer

Tejal Daruwale Soni

Graphics

Kirk D'Penha

Production Coordinator

Shraddha Falebhai

About the Author

Fernando J Miguel has been working with software development since 2003 and has continued researching methods to improve his skills through hard work and commitment. He has worked with CMS since 2004 and Magento, specifically, since 2009.

A Certified Professional Scrum Master by the Scrum Alliance, he loves to apply agile as a way of life and improves himself to achieve excellence in work and customers and team satisfaction. He has a background on different technologies and is always seeking the best solution for the current project.

As a University professor, he motivates students to find their own paths and seek excellence in their professional IT careers.

Fernando has a bachelor's degree in Information Systems (Módulo University – Caraguatatuba/SP – Brazil). He has post graduated in Project Management/PMI-PMBOK (Cruzeiro do Sul University – São Paulo/SP – Brazil).

He worked as a Technical Reviewer for *Magento 1.4 Theming cookbook, Mastering Magento, Mastering Magento [Video], Mastering Magento Theme Design.*

He was the Author of *Magento 2 Development Essentials (2016).*

> *I dedicate all my work to my brother Wagner for all the support. Without family support, I never could be here. Thank you to all my family.*

About the Reviewer

Richard Carter is a seasoned front-end web developer who has worked with Magento since 2008. He lives in Newcastle upon Tyne in the North East of England.

He is the founder of the e-commerce agency Peacock Carter, an e-commerce and web design agency based in the North East of England, and has worked for clients including the Scottish Government, City & Guilds, NHS, and the University of Edinburgh.

Richard is the author of four books on Magento, including *Magento Responsive Theme Design*, and has written three further books on e-commerce and content management systems.

Thanks to Gillian, who is forever at my side.

www.PacktPub.com

For support files and downloads related to your book, please visit www.PacktPub.com.

Did you know that Packt offers eBook versions of every book published, with PDF and ePub files available? You can upgrade to the eBook version at www.PacktPub.com and as a print book customer, you are entitled to a discount on the eBook copy. Get in touch with us at service@packtpub.com for more details.

At www.PacktPub.com, you can also read a collection of free technical articles, sign up for a range of free newsletters and receive exclusive discounts and offers on Packt books and eBooks.

https://www.packtpub.com/mapt

Get the most in-demand software skills with Mapt. Mapt gives you full access to all Packt books and video courses, as well as industry-leading tools to help you plan your personal development and advance your career.

Why subscribe?

- Fully searchable across every book published by Packt
- Copy and paste, print, and bookmark content
- On demand and accessible via a web browser

To my grandmother Mildes and my mother Edneia, wherever they are, I'm sure they are very happy with my work. To my beloved wife Elizabete for the countless hours of patience with my work. Love you.

Table of Contents

Preface

Digital buyers are increasing the economy around the world, and Information Technology (IT) is providing the necessary subsidies to allow the customers to buy services and products over the Internet. According to the research conducted by Statista (`http://goo.gl/BSCiuO`), in 2016, 1.12 billion people worldwide are expected to buy goods and services online.

Since the launch of Amazon.com, the first commercial-free 24-hour e-commerce website, the universe of software development's techniques have evolved and new approaches are emerging, such as cloud computing: previously, an embryonic idea, today a concrete application.

The Magento Commerce company, recognized as the leading e-commerce platform in the 2015 Internet Retailer Top 1000, B2B 300, and Hot 100 lists, is in constant evolution since the first Magento Community Edition (CE) system version in 2008. Launched recently, Magento CE 2.0 has great features and takes advantage of the newest client-server techniques, providing a mature e-commerce system and a promising professional area to explore.

Magento CE 2.0 works with a modern theming and layout framework, extensive and efficient APIs, stable interfaces with the business logic layer and, mainly, a reliable system to allow the implementation of custom functionalities.

Magento 2 Theme Development covers the newest concepts in Magento theme development. The mission of this book is to give to the readers the necessary information to start mastering the Magento Theme Development concepts.

Enjoy the read.

What this book covers

Chapter 1, *Introduction to Magento 2*, introduces you to the basic concepts of Magento 2, shows the Magento websites that are on the market, and guides you through building a local development environment Magento 2.

Chapter 2, *Exploring Magento Themes*, teaches you the structure of the themes in Magento 2, as well as the importance of the Luma and Blank themes.

Chapter 3, *Magento 2 Theme Layout*, shows you how to work with the Model-View-Controller architecture, the command-line interface, the layout system, and theme debuging.

Chapter 4, *Magento UI Library*, teaches you how to use the Magento UI library, LESS compilation, and CSS preprocessing.

Chapter 5, *Creating a Responsive Magento 2 Theme*, guides you to the development of a new theme for Magento 2.

Chapter 6, *Magento 2 Styles Debugging*, teaches you how to create a flow to test your styles, client-side debugging, server-side debugging, and the Grunt task runner.

Chapter 7, *Magento UI Components*, teaches you how to work with UI components: listing, grid, a form.

Chapter 8, *Magento Layout Development*, shows you the layout instructions, and the types, and techniques required to customize your template.

Chapter 9, *Magento 2 JavaScript*, teaches you how to work with JavaScript in Magento and jQuery widgets by developing a simple extension.

Chapter 10, *Social Media in Magento 2*, guides you through the development of a new extension that integrates Magento 2 with social media.

Chapter 11, *Theme Development Best Practices*, shows you the best practices of developing themes for Magento 2.

Chapter 12, *Magento Theme Distribution*, shows you an overview of the packaging process to sell and share your developed theme.

What you need for this book

The following software is recommended for maximum enjoyment:

- Linux, OSX, or Windows (7, 8, or 10)
- XAMPP
- Browser (Google Chrome or Firefox)
- Code editor (Sublime Text, Notepad++, or Atom.io)

Who this book is for

This book is for web developers, Magento developers, and students who want to work with Magento 2. This book builds a solid path to follow that will help you master the concepts of theme development in Magento 2.

Conventions

In this book, you will find a number of styles of text that distinguish between different kinds of information. Here are some examples of these styles, and an explanation of their meaning.

Code words in text, database table names, folder names, filenames, file extensions, pathnames, dummy URLs, user input, and Twitter handles are shown as follows: "Log in as $var and enter the password you chose earlier with config."

A block of code is set as follows:

```php
<?php
\Magento\Framework\Component\ComponentRegistrar::register(
    \Magento\Framework\Component\ComponentRegistrar::MODULE,
    'Packt_SweetTweet',
    __DIR__
);
```

Any command-line input or output is written as follows:

```
packt@magento ~ $ grunt clean
```

New terms and important words are shown in bold. Words that you see on the screen, for example, in menus or dialog boxes, appear in the text like this: "Clicking the **Next** button moves you to the next screen."

Warnings or important notes appear in a box like this.

Tips and tricks appear like this.

Reader feedback

Feedback from our readers is always welcome. Let us know what you think about this book—what you liked or disliked. Reader feedback is important for us as it helps us develop titles that you will really get the most out of.

To send us general feedback, simply e-mail `feedback@packtpub.com`, and mention the book's title in the subject of your message.

If there is a topic that you have expertise in and you are interested in either writing or contributing to a book, see our author guide at `www.packtpub.com/authors`.

Customer support

Now that you are the proud owner of a Packt book, we have a number of things to help you to get the most from your purchase.

Downloading the example code

You can download the example code files for this book from your account at `http://www.packtpub.com`. If you purchased this book elsewhere, you can visit `http://www.packtpub.com/support` and register to have the files e-mailed directly to you.

You can download the code files by following these steps:

1. Log in or register to our website using your e-mail address and password.
2. Hover the mouse pointer on the **SUPPORT** tab at the top.
3. Click on **Code Downloads & Errata**.
4. Enter the name of the book in the **Search** box.
5. Select the book for which you're looking to download the code files.
6. Choose from the drop-down menu where you purchased this book from.
7. Click on **Code Download**.

You can also download the code files by clicking on the **Code Files** button on the book's webpage at the Packt Publishing website. This page can be accessed by entering the book's name in the Search box. Please note that you need to be logged in to your Packt account.

Once the file is downloaded, please make sure that you unzip or extract the folder using the latest version of:

- WinRAR / 7-Zip for Windows
- Zipeg / iZip / UnRarX for Mac
- 7-Zip / PeaZip for Linux

The code bundle for the book is also hosted on GitHub at `https://github.com/PacktPublishing/Magento-2-Theme-Design`. We also have other code bundles from our rich catalog of books and videos available at `https://github.com/PacktPublishing/`. Check them out!

Errata

Although we have taken every care to ensure the accuracy of our content, mistakes do happen. If you find a mistake in one of our books—maybe a mistake in the text or the code—we would be grateful if you could report this to us. By doing so, you can save other readers from frustration and help us improve subsequent versions of this book. If you find any errata, please report them by visiting `http://www.packtpub.com/submit-errata`, selecting your book, clicking on the Errata Submission Form link, and entering the details of your errata. Once your errata are verified, your submission will be accepted and the errata will be uploaded to our website or added to any list of existing errata under the Errata section of that title.

To view the previously submitted errata, go to `https://www.packtpub.com/books/content/support` and enter the name of the book in the search field. The required information will appear under the Errata section.

Piracy

Piracy of copyrighted material on the Internet is an ongoing problem across all media. At Packt, we take the protection of our copyright and licenses very seriously. If you come across any illegal copies of our works in any form on the Internet, please provide us with the location address or website name immediately so that we can pursue a remedy.

Please contact us at copyright@packtpub.com with a link to the suspected pirated material.

We appreciate your help in protecting our authors and our ability to bring you valuable content.

Questions

If you have a problem with any aspect of this book, you can contact us at questions@packtpub.com, and we will do our best to address the problem.

1
Introduction to Magento 2

"Computers themselves, and software yet to be developed, will revolutionize the way we learn" – Steve Jobs.

The Internet is an important sector of many businesses, both large and small, in the modern world. It's now rare for a company to not have at least a basic web presence, and increasingly unlikely that a company's products are not sold online. **Magento** is a powerful e-commerce system, used by international organizations such as Nike, Nestlé, Gant, and Fun4Kids.

This is what we will see in this chapter:

- Take a look at what Magento 2 is and what it can do
- Discover the differences between Magento 1.x and Magento 2.x
- See the default themes that come installed with Magento 2.x
- Look at a showcase of custom Magento themes from real websites
- Find out the particular challenges in customizing Magento themes
- Install and configure Magento 2 ready for theming

As you will come to see, Magento is quite a large e-commerce system and this book will guide you through customizing its quirks and eccentricities.

What is Magento?

Magento (`http://www.magentocommerce.com`) is a highly customizable e-commerce platform and content management system. Magento is one of the most widely used e-commerce systems to create online stores around the world by providing management of inventory, orders, customers, payments, and much more. Magento has a powerful scalable architecture that follows the best software development patterns on the market. Take a look at the following screenshot:

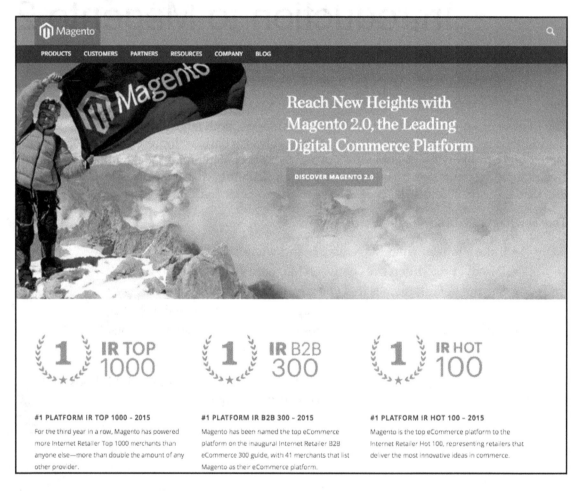

Magento is written in the PHP programming language using an object-orientated architecture, allowing features such as additional payment gateways, integration with social networks such as Twitter and Facebook, and customization for different product types to be easily added.

The default installation of Magento provides a huge number of e-commerce and related features, supports multiple stores being managed from the same control panel, and importantly for us—provides the ability for very heavily customized themes.

At the beginning, Magento was very criticized for being slow when loading its pages, which could be at least partially mitigated with the use of built-in caches. However, in Magento 2 we have a considerable evolution on system performance with the adoption of the **LESS** preprocessor, **Full Page Caching, Indexers Optimization**, and the adoption of new techniques and technologies, as you will see in the following chapters.

Magento 2's features

As with other e-commerce systems, Magento allows products to be added, edited, manipulated, and organized within categories. You are able to control your product's names, descriptions, prices, and upload multiple photographs for each product in your store. Magento also lets you create variations of products in your store, so you can have one product that is available in multiple colors (such as blue, red, and black) within Magento. In other e-commerce systems, you may have to add the blue, red, and black products as three separate products.

In addition to these *standard* e-commerce features, Magento also has the ability to perform the following:

- Manage both the sending of e-mail newsletters and the managing of subscribers to these lists
- Manage non-product pages through its **content management system** (**CMS**)
- Organize polls of your store's visitors

Additional features are available in **Magento Enterprise Edition**, but this book concentrates on **Magento 2 Community Edition**; everything in this book can be applied to all editions of Magento 2.

Differences between Magento 1 and Magento 2

There are some fairly major differences between Magento 1 and Magento 2. Magento 2 provides major updates on its previous version after some hard work to create the best solutions to old issues such as performance and security. The updates can be illustrated by the following list:

- **Caching**: There's a built-in **Full Page Cache** (**FPC**) on the Community Edition and **Varnish** support for improved performance.
- **Extensions and Themes**: Magento 2 is more organized and extensible now. The extensions and themes have your own files of code and layout.
- **File structure**: More organized directories and structures inside the **Model View-Controller** (**MVC**) proposal.
- **Performance**: Improved performance and scalability.
- **Security**: Enhancements in security with the adoption of good software development practices (design patterns) and **SHA-256** password hashing included.
- **User Experience** (**UX**): Besides the frontend changes, the Magento 2 admin area is now more user-friendly with substantial positive changes such as the new admin area structure and management.

Magento 2, compared with Magento 1.9, shows some changes, but more than that, there is an improvement in the system's behavior and processes. The code is more organized; it separates the Magento framework's native extensions, providing a powerful environment for modularization and solution development:

The main changes in the structure of Magento 2 are as follows:

- The `skin` directory does not exist anymore. All the files of a module or theme are stored in its specific scope.
- The native modules and themes of Magento 2 installation are in the vendor directory.
- The `pub` directory contains all the CSS and PHTML files precompiled.
- The `composer.json` file manages the project dependencies.

> For further information about the Magento 2 directory structure, please access `http://devdocs.magento.com/guides/v2.0/extension-dev-gui de/module-file-structure.html`.

In Magento 1, the theme system works by rendering the layout files (PHTML) from the `app/design/frontend/MyTheme` directory and by rendering the CSS, JS, and Image files from the `skin/frontend/MyTheme` directory. However, in Magento 2, all the layout and CSS files are in the same directory, `Theme`.

The themes of Magento 2 are located in the `app/design/frontend/<Vendor>/` directory. This location differs with built-in themes, such as the **Luma** theme, which is located in `vendor/magento/theme-frontend-luma`.

The different themes are stored in separate directories:

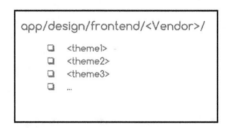

Each `Vendor` can have one or more themes attached to it, so you can develop different themes inside the same `Vendor`.

The theme structure of Magento 2 is illustrated as follows:

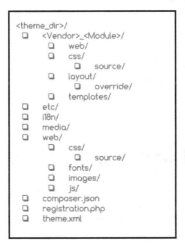

```
<theme_dir>/
    □    <Vendor>_<Module>/
              □    web/
              □    css/
                        □    source/
              □    layout/
                        □    override/
              □    templates/
    □    etc/
    □    i18n/
    □    media/
    □    web/
              □    css/
                        □    source/
              □    fonts/
              □    images/
              □    js/
    □    composer.json
    □    registration.php
    □    theme.xml
```

How Magento.2's theme structure works is quite simple to understand: each `<Vendor>_<Module>` corresponds a specific module or functionality of your theme. For example, `Magento_Customer` has specific CSS and HTML files to handle the customer module of the Magento vendor. Magento handles a significant number of modules. So, I strongly suggest you navigate to the `vendor/magento/theme-frontend-luma` folder to see the available modules for the default theme.

In the structure of Magento 2, we have three main files that manage the themes' behavior:

- `composer.json`: Describes the dependencies and meta information
- `registration.php`: Registers your theme in the system
- `theme.xml`: Declares the theme in the system and is used by the Magento system to recognize the theme

All the theme files, inside the structure explained in the previous section, can be divided into **Static View Files** and **Dynamic View Files**. The Static View Files are not processed by the server (images, fonts, js) and the Dynamic View Files are processed by the server before delivering the content to the user (template and layout files).

Static files generally are published in the following folders:

- /pub/static/frontend/<Vendor>/<theme>/<language>
- <theme_dir>/media/
- <theme_dir>/web

For further information, please access the official Magento Theme structure documentation: `http://goo.gl/ov3IUJ`

In `Chapter 2`, *Exploring Magento Themes*, you will see this structure in action by exploring the default themes of Magento 2. Now, let's take a look at a showcase of running Magento 2 solutions.

Showcase of Magento themes

There is a plethora of e-commerce websites that make use of Magento, and some of them truly demonstrate how flexible Magento can be when it comes to theming. Here is a selection of live Magento stores that really push the platform beyond the typical Magento themes you've already seen.

Venroy

Venroy is a menswear department store in Australia. Their Magento 2 store (`https://www.venroy.com.au`) follows the basic Magento 2 design principles and **RWD** design:

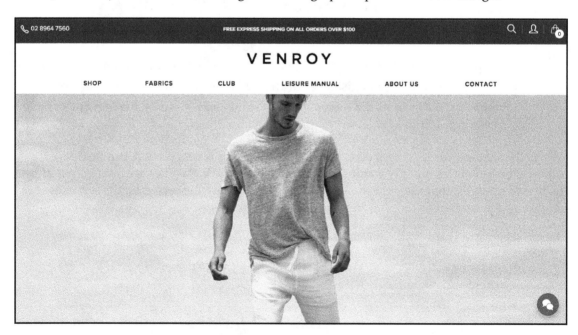

The store's homepage was built in a different way compared to the Luma default theme available in Magento 2. The primary navigation of the Venroy website, for example, is displayed in the top-center of the screen and it makes it highly visible to customers.

When interacted with, the store's category view expands to display more specific sub-categories:

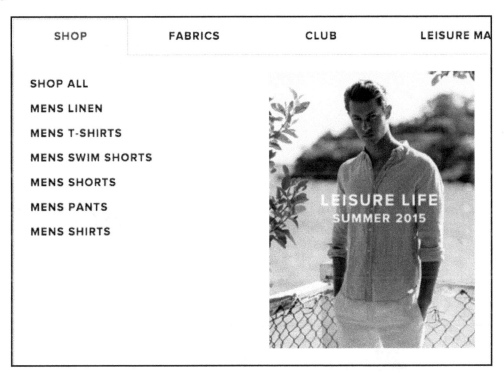

The product detail view is also heavily customized, with information on the product, delivery, and size guides all provided with their own separate blocks:

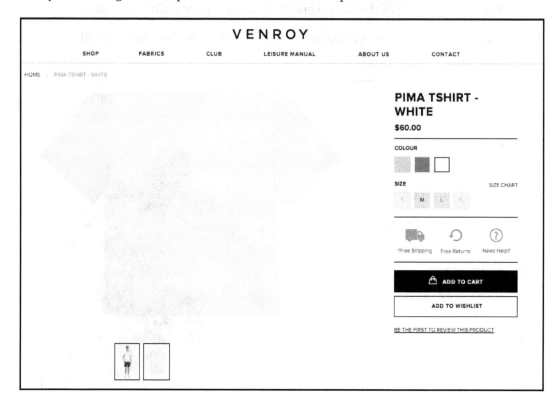

Alcatel Onetouch

Alcatel Onetouch (`http://www.alcatelonetouch.us/`) is an international mobile technology brand that adopts Magento 2 to sell its products:

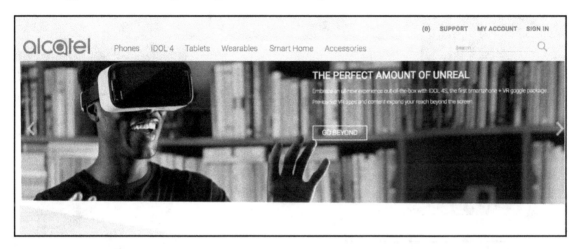

As you can see, the homepage is quite heavily customized, with the featured products displayed on the homepage.

The product detail page, which is part of the Magento store, is similarly styled in an appealing way, with plenty of screen space given to information such as the product reviews, details, technical specifications, and manual:

Cultcha Kids

Cultcha Kids (https://www.cultchakids.com.au/) is a toy store, and is therefore, focused on a younger audience, with specific and famous brands:

The product detail page is fully customized to the store's purposes and audience, as you can see in the following screenshot:

Challenges of Magento 2 theme design

Magento 2 is a comprehensive and, at times, complex system, and this is reflected in some of the challenges that designers come across when creating themes for Magento 2:

- **Complexity**: As Magento 2 is a large system, it can initially be infuriating to create themes with, though after some time you should become more familiar with Magento's inner workings
- **Breadth of knowledge**: Magento 2 theming involves tackling a mixture of XML (for layout files), CSS (for style), (X)HTML, and snippets of PHP (for the templates)

Why create a custom Magento 2 theme?

There are a number of reasons why you may want to create or customize a Magento 2 theme:

- The first and most obvious reason to customize your Magento 2 theme is that this can help you to distinguish your store from your competitors.
- Customizing your Magento 2 theme can also allow you to better integrate extensions from Magento Connect into your store, with additional features.
- If you have an existing website and wish to add e-commerce by integrating Magento 2 around the existing system, theming Magento 2 can make sure that there is visually seamless integration between the two systems.
- Theming Magento 2 can also be useful in order to customize your store to reflect the different expectations of your customers from around the world. For example, customers in some countries may expect components of your store to appear in one location on their screen, so you could theme Magento 2 to reflect this if your customers are primarily from that country.

Installing Magento 2

Before we get started with customizing the look and feel of our Magento store, you will need to install Magento 2.

XAMPP PHP development environment

There are great options in the market to help us create the local development environment to work with Magento 2:

- **XAMPP** (https://www.apachefriends.org/)
- **LAMP** (https://www.turnkeylinux.org/lampstack/)
- **MAMP** (https://www.mamp.info/en/)
- **Vagrant** (https://www.vagrantup.com/)

You can feel free to choose your option to use as a solution. In this book, will be suggesting using of XAMPP.

XAMPP is a complete web development environment. In its install package you can find **Apache**, **MySQL**, **PHP**, and **Perl**: everything that you want to develop your solutions.

You may be able to guess the meaning of XAMPP, but the X before the AMPP means cross or cross-platform. So, we have: Cross-platform, Apache, Maria DB, PHP, and Perl.

The goal of XAMPP is to build an easy-to-install distribution for developers to get into the world of Apache. XAMPP is a project of **Apache Friends**, a non-profit project to promote Apache Web Server.

But why are we working with this software? Let's find out:

- **Apache** (`http://httpd.apache.org/`) has been the most popular web server on the Internet since April 1995, providing secure, efficient, and extensible HTTP services in sync with the current HTTP standards.
- **MariaDB** (`https://mariadb.org/`), strives to be the logical choice for database professionals looking for a robust, scalable, and reliable SQL server.
- **PHP** (`http://php.net/`) is a popular general-purpose scripting language that is especially suited to web development and, most importantly, it is the main language of Magento.
- **Perl** (`https://www.perl.org/`) is a highly capable, feature-rich programming language with over 27 years of development.

So far so good, but how about doing some action?

XAMPP installation

First of all, let's access the XAMPP website at its URL, `https://www.apachefriends.org`:

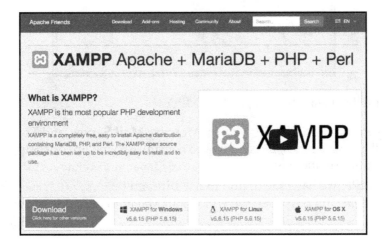

XAMPP has three distinct versions for different **operating systems** (**OS**es): Windows, Linux, and OS X. Choose your preferred version to download and start the installation process.

XAMPP for Windows installation

XAMPP for Windows has three different kinds of installation files:

- **Installer**: Classic Windows installation
- **Zip**: Compressed files to install manually
- **7zip**: Compressed files to install manually

The **Installer** (.exe) is the most popular process to install. Please download it and execute to start the installation process:

The following are the installation steps of XAMPP:

1. You can skip **FileZilla Ftp Server**, **Mercury Mail Server**, and **Tomcat** for our installation purposes, but feel free to consult Apache Friends Support Forum for further information: https://community.apachefriends.org.
2. In XAMPP, we have the option to use **Bitnami** (https://bitnami.com/xampp), but for learning purposes, we will install Magento in the classic way.

3. Complete the installation by pressing the **Finish** button:

4. In order to start XAMPP for Windows, you can execute `xampp-control.exe` and start the Apache Web Server.

5. To test if everything is working, type `http://localhost` in your favorite web browser. You should see the XAMPP start page:

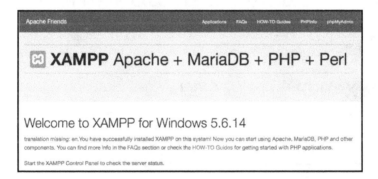

XAMPP for Linux installation

XAMPP for Linux has two main versions of the installation file:

- 32-bit version
- 64-bit version

Choose the file according to your architecture and follow these steps:

1. Change the permissions to the installer:

   ```
   chmod 755 xampp-linux-*-installer.run
   ```

2. Run the installer:

   ```
   sudo ./xampp-linux-*-installer.run
   ```

XAMPP is now installed in the /opt/lampp directory.

To start XAMPP, execute this command in the terminal:

```
sudo /opt/lampp/lampp start
```

To test if everything is working, type http://localhost in your favorite web browser and you should see the XAMPP start page:

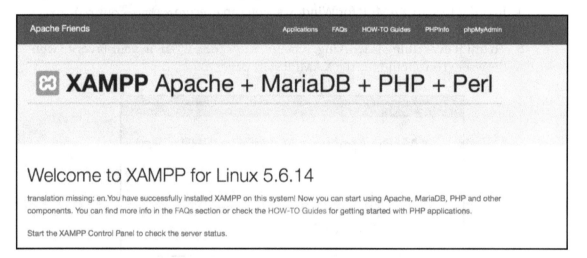

XAMPP for OS X installation

To install XAMPP for OS X you simply follow these steps:

1. Download the DMG-Image file.
2. Open the image file to start the installation process.
3. The steps are pretty much the same as Windows installation, refer to the section *XAMPP for Windows installation*.

4. To test if everything is working, type `http://localhost` in your favorite web browser. You should see the XAMPP start page:

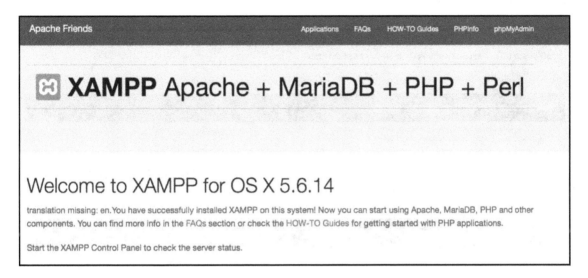

The XAMPP `htdocs` directory is the `docroot` folder of your server. Everything that you save in the `htdocs` folder, you can access via the browser. For example, if you save `index.php` inside `htdocs`, you can access this script by entering this URL: `http://localhost/index.php`. If you save your file in the `packt` directory, you can access it by going to `http://localhost/packt/index.php`. Piece of cake!

Downloading Magento 2

First of all, we need to create a user on the Magento website (`http://www.magento.com`). To download **Magento 2 Community Edition**, click on **My Account**, and after clicking the button labeled **Register**, fill in the form and confirm your registration.

Once registered, you will be able to download Magento 2. Access the **Products** menu, **Open Source/CE**, and finally **View Available Downloads** (`https://www.magentocommerce.com/download`):

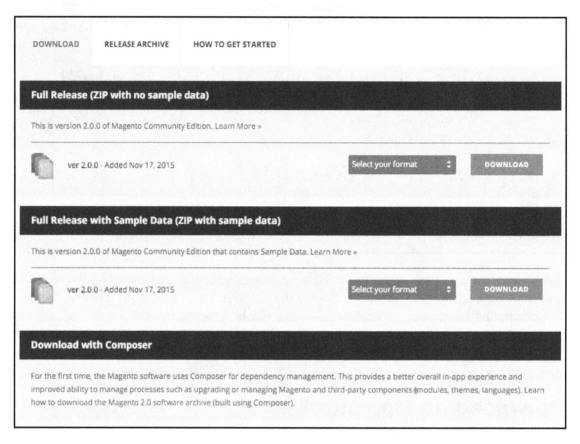

On this page, we have three important options:

- **Full Release (ZIP with no sample data)**: The download of the last and stable Magento version
- **Full Release with Sample Data (ZIP with sample data)**: This is important for creating example products for our store for testing
- **Download with Composer**: This is the dependency management installation tool

Please choose **Full Release with Sample Data** to download. Extract the compressed files in the `XAMPP htdocs` directory and rename the new directory `packt`.

Remember to start the Apache and MySQL services on the XAMPP panel before the installation of Magento 2.

Before we start our Magento installation, we'll need to create a new MySQL database instance to store the Magento data. **phpMyAdmin** is a MySQL web app to manage your database:

1. Please access `http://localhost/phpmyadmin/`.

2. Click on the **Databases** menu and the **Create database** option and create a database called `packt`, as shown in the following screenshot:

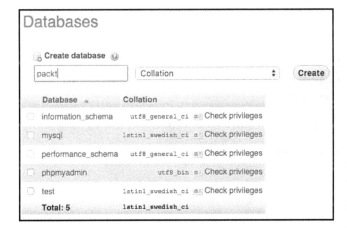

3. Access the following URL, `http://localhost/packt/setup`, to start the Magento installation.

By this point, you can see this installation page on your browser:

Let's start Magento installation by following these steps:

1. **Readiness Check**: Check the environment for the correct PHP version, PHP extensions, file permissions, and compatibility.
2. **Add a Database**: Fill in the database form with your connection information. By default, you can follow the suggestions. Take a look at the following screenshot:

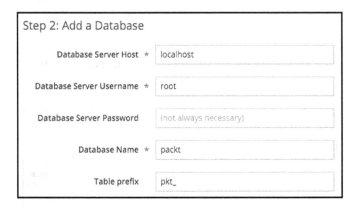

3. **Web Configuration**: **Your Store Address** and **Magento Admin Address**.

4. **Customize Your Store**: Time zone, currency, and language information:

5. **Create Admin Account**: Enter your personal login information and set the admin
   address to `admin_packt`.

After following these steps, you have Magento 2 running! You can access your new site by
going to `http://localhost/packt`:

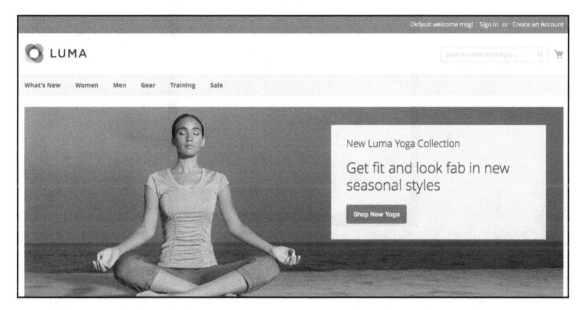

And you can access the admin area by going to `http://localhost/packt/admin_packt:`

For further information about Magento installation, please go to `http://d evdocs.magento.com/guides/v2.0/install-gde/bk-install-guide.ht ml`

Summary

You've now seen what Magento can do, and the changes and improvements in this newer version of Magento 2. Perhaps more importantly, we've installed Magento 2 too, so it's ready to starting theming! The remainder of this book covers customizing your Magento 2 theme, from the basics, such as changing your store's logos and color schemes, to e-mail templates, and more.

2
Exploring Magento Themes

"It's an up and down thing, the human goals, because the human is always an explorer, an adventurist" – Cesar Millan

As you've already seen, Magento 2 can be a complex platform to customize, so this chapter will help you to explore Magento 2 themes, including the following:

- Magento terminology
- What a Magento theme is: the elements that comprise a Magento 2 theme
- Theme hierarchy in Magento 2
- Magento's Blank and Luma themes
- Installing and activating a Magento 2 theme

Magento terminology

Before you look at Magento themes, it's beneficial to know the difference between what Magento calls vendors and what Magento calls themes and the distinguishing factors of websites and stores.

Magento vendors and themes

According to the official documentation, a Magento theme is a component that provides a visual design for an entire application area using a combination of custom templates, layouts, styles, or images. Themes are implemented by different vendors and are intended to be distributed as additional packages for Magento, similar to other components.

Each vendor can have one or more themes attached to it, so you can develop different themes inside the same vendor:

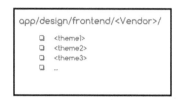

Each theme can have specific rules and custom layout files providing better flexibility both for administrators and developers. The Magento 2 theme structure can be described as follows:

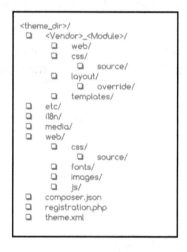

The way that Magento's theme structure works is quite simple. Each `<Vendor>_<Module>` corresponds a specific module or functionality of your theme. For example, `Magento_Customer` has specific CSS and HTML files to handle the customer module of the Magento vendor. Magento handles a significant number of modules.

I strongly suggest you navigate to the `vendor/magento/theme-frontend-luma` directory to see the available modules for the default theme. In the Magento 2 structure, we have three main files that manage the behavior of themes:

- `composer.json`: Describes the dependencies and meta information
- `registration.php`: Registers your theme on the system
- `theme.xml`: Declares the theme on the system and is used by the Magento system to recognize the theme

All the theme files inside the structure explained in the previous section can be divided into **Static View Files** and **Dynamic View Files**. Static View Files are not processed by the server (images, fonts, js) and Dynamic View Files are processed by the server before delivering the content to the user (template and layout files).

Static view files generally are published in the following directories:

- `/pub/static/frontend/<Vendor>/<theme>/<language>`
- `<theme_dir>/media/`
- `<theme_dir>/web`

 For further information, please access the official Magento theme structure documentation at `http://goo.gl/ov3IUJ`.

Magento websites and Magento stores

The terms **websites** and **stores** have a slightly different meaning in Magento than in general and in other systems. For example, if your business is called **PacktPub**, you might have three Magento stores (managed through the same installation of Magento) with the following names:

- **Book Store**
- **Mag Store**
- **Media Store**

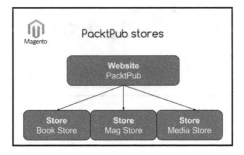

In this case, Magento refers to **PacktPub** as the **Website** and the stores are **Book Store**, **Mag Store**, and **Media Store**. Each store then has one or more store views associated with it, too. The simplest Magento website consists of a store and store view (usually of the same name):

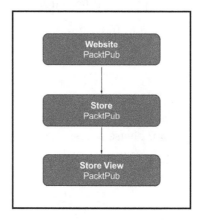

A slightly more complex Magento store may just have one store view for each store. This is a useful technique if you want to manage more than one store in the same Magento installation, with each store selling different products (for example, the Blue Store sells blue products and the Yellow Store sells yellow products):

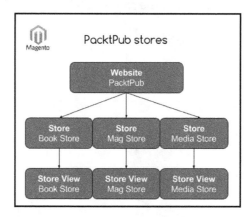

If a store were to make use of more than one Magento store view, it might be to present customers with a bilingual website. For example, our **Book Store** may have an **English**, **Spanish**, and **Japanese** store view associated with it:

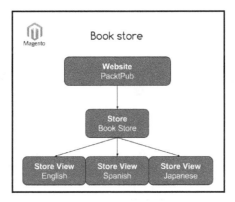

Let's now create this website and stores setup in our Magento admin area by following this recipe:

1. Open your favorite browser and log in to the admin area (`http://localhost/packt/admin_packt`).
2. Navigate to **Stores | All Stores**.
3. Click on the **Create Website** button, set as default, and save the new website with the name `Packtpub` and code `packtpub`.
4. Click on the **Create Stores** button to create three stores, one at a time: the Book Store, Mag Store, and Media Store, which belong to the Packtpub website.
5. Click on the **Create Store View** button to create three store views, one at a time: **English**, **Japanese**, and **Spanish**, which all belong to **Book Store**.

Take a look at the following screenshot:

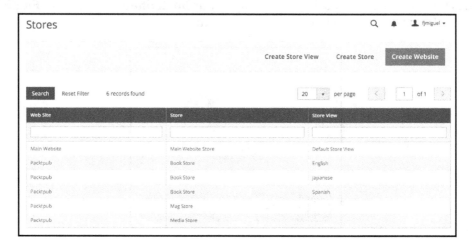

Now Magento has three stores and three different views of **Book Store**. To test the views, navigate to the homepage (`http://localhost/packt`) and access the store view menu in the upper-right corner:

For further information, please refer to the *Magento 2 CE Edition – User Guide* document available at `http://goo.gl/Naew9J`.

What makes a Magento theme?

A Magento theme is a collection of files that define the look, layout, and other outputs from the Magento system.

Unique aspects of a Magento theme

Magento 2 themes differ from design implementations in other content management systems and e-commerce platforms in a few key ways:

- Maximum ability to customize Magento
- Support for multiple concurrent themes
- They offer an uninterrupted workflow
- They minimize debugging time for errors

Magento's theming system provides the ability to highly customize the way Magento 2 looks to your customers: you can customize every aspect of your Magento store through layout, CSS, JavaScript, templates, and local files.

The support for multiple concurrent themes is another feature that makes Magento somewhat unique in its field, allowing you to style your store differently with Magento.

Default Magento 2 themes

By default, Magento 2 comes with two different themes:

1. **Luma**: Created with the purpose to initiate the understanding of Magento 2's theme structure. It's highly recommended not to use this as your production theme.
2. **Blank**: Provides the basic theme structure, used as a boilerplate to develop new themes in Magento 2.

You can easily preview the Luma theme on the Magento demonstration site at `http://demo2.aheadworks.com`, provided by **aheadWorks** Company (`http://www.aheadworks.com`).

Magento Luma theme

The Luma theme implements **responsive web design** (**RWD**) as a good practice to use in theme development, and inherits code and layout from the **Blank** theme. The Magento 2 Blank theme, found in the `vendor/magento/theme-frontend-blank` folder, is the basic Magento theme and is declared as the parent theme of Luma. How is it possible? Logically, Magento has distinct folders for every theme, but Magento is very smart and reuses code. Magento takes advantage of theme inheritance. You will see more about theme inheritance in the next chapter.

The Luma theme is what you see when you install Magento 2. The homepage is based upon a one-column structure:

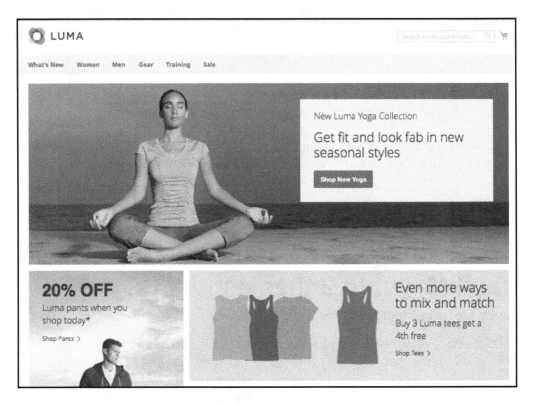

In the preceding screenshot, you can see that the Luma theme works with good design principles through a distinction between each section and product promotions used for content. The categories and the shopping cart icon are at the top of the page. Near the bottom, we have the **Hot Sellers** section, which provides some available products. Finally, the bottom of the page provides some additional information, such as an **About us** link.

Product pages display pictures of featured products in a two column layout:

On the product page, you can see options such as **Compare Products** and **Wish List**, a breadcrumb trail to where the page is located within your store's hierarchy, as well as photographs of the product, which can be enlarged:

LifeLong Fitness IV

Be the first to review this product

$14.00

IN STOCK
SKU#: 240-LV05

Trailers

Trailer #1

Trailer #2

Trailer #3

The instructors and routines featured in LifeLong Fitness IV provide safe options to serve all types of physical conditions and abilities. Range of motion, body awareness and breathing practices are essential tools of yogic self-care, essential for maintaining alertness, health, and dignity over a lifetime. The LifeLong Fitness series acknowledges that as we age, the safety and sustainability of our exercise become as important as pushing our limits.

$14.00

The category page reverts to a two-column layout, presenting products as a grid by default. As is common across many Magento themes, you're able to view products in two distinct ways. The grid view displays the products in a grid:

The list view allows more information about the products to be displayed alongside the product photograph and other information shown in the grid view:

The Luma theme's style is based on the Magento **user interface** (**UI**) library and uses **CSS3** media queries to work with screen width, adapting the layout according to the device that accesses it. In the next chapter, we will see how Magento's UI works.

Magento Blank theme

The Blank theme provides all the conceivable files that a Magento store requires to run without error, so that the new custom themes built will not cause errors if a file does not exist within it.

The Blank theme does not contain all of the CSS and images required to style your store, as you'll be doing this with our custom theme.

Don't change the Magento vendor package!
It is important that you do not edit any files in the vendor/magento package and that you do not attempt to create a custom theme in the vendor directory, as this will make fully upgrading Magento difficult. Make sure any custom themes you are working on are within their own design package; for example, your theme's files should be located in app/design/frontend/<Vendor>/.

Blocks and pages in Magento

Magento uses **blocks** to differentiate between the various components of its functionality, the idea being that this makes it easier for Magento developers and Magento theme designers to customize the functionality of Magento and the look and feel of Magento respectively.

A **content block** displays the generated HTML provided by Magento for any given feature. Content blocks are used *within* Magento structural blocks. Examples of content blocks in Magento include the following:

- The search feature
- Product listings
- The mini cart
- Category listings
- Site navigation links
- Callouts (advertising blocks)

Simply, content blocks are the *what* of a Magento theme: they define what type of content appears within any given page or view within Magento.

Usually, the blocks are available in a visual hierarchy from a page. A typical structure of a three-column block in a Magento theme includes the following:

- **Header**
- **Primary area**
- **Left column**
- **Right column**
- **Footer**

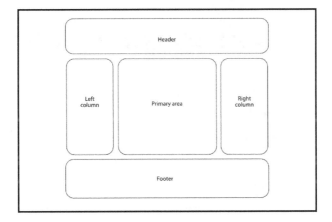

Magento has a flexible theme system. Beyond Magento code customization, the admin can create blocks and content on the Magento admin panel such as **Home** page and **About Us**; any static page that you want to create. **CMS (Content Management System)** pages and blocks on Magento give you the power to embed HTML code in your page.

You can create or edit pages and blocks by accessing the **Admin** area
(`http://localhost/packt/admin_packt`) and navigating to **Content** | **Pages**:

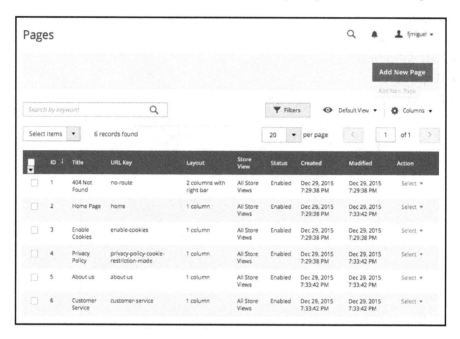

Magento theme inheritance

The frontend of Magento allows designers to create new themes based on the basic Blank
theme, reusing the main code without changing its main structure. The fallback system is a
theme's inheritance mechanism and allows the developers to create only the files that are
necessary for customization.

The Luma theme, for example, uses the fallback system by inheriting the Blank theme's
basic structure. The Luma theme's parent is declared in its `theme.xml` file:

```
<theme xmlns:xsi="http://www.w3.org/2001/XMLSchema-instance"
xsi:noNamespaceSchemaLocation="urn:magento:framework:Config/etc/theme.xsd">
    <title>Magento Luma</title>
    <parent>Magento/blank</parent>
    <media>
        <preview_image>media/preview.jpg</preview_image>
    </media>
</theme>
```

The inheritance works like an override system. You can create new themes by using the existent ones (parents) and by replacing (overriding) some existing file with the same name, but in your specific theme folder (child).

For example, if you create a new theme in folder `app/design/frontend/<Vendor>/<theme>/` and declares **Magento/blank** as a parent theme, `theme.xml` file and `registration.php`, you have the entire blank theme structure ready to work in your new theme including RWD layouts and styles.

Let's say that you have a specific CSS available in the `<theme_dir>/web/css` folder. If you delete this file, the fallback system will search the file in the `<parent_theme_dir>/web/css` folder:

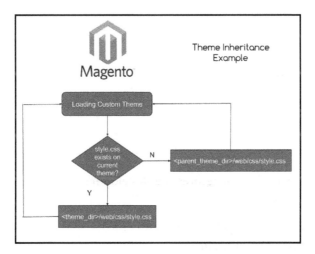

Custom Variables

Custom Variables are pieces of code that have specific values, like a programming variable. By creating a Custom Variable, you can apply it to multiple areas on your site. An example of Custom Variable structure is `{{config path="web/unsecure/base_url"}}`. This variable shows the URL of the store.

Now let's create a Custom Variable to see how it works:

1. Open your favorite browser and access the admin area, `http://localhost/packt/admin_packt`.
2. Navigate to **System | Custom Variables**.

3. Click on the **Add New Variable** button.
4. In the **Variable Code** field, enter the variable in lowercase and with no spaces, for example, `dev_name`.
5. Enter **Variable Name**, which explains the variable's purpose.
6. Enter the **Variable HTML Value** and **Variable Plain Value** of the Custom Variable and save it.

Now we have a custom variable that stores the developer's name. Let's use this variable inside the CMS **About Us** page:

1. In the admin area, navigate to **Content | Pages**.
2. Click to edit the **About Us** item.
3. Click on the **Content** side menu.
4. Click on the **Show / Hide Editor** button to hide the HTML editor.

5. Put the following code at the end of the content, `{{CustomVar code="dev_name"}}`, and save the content.

Let's check the result:

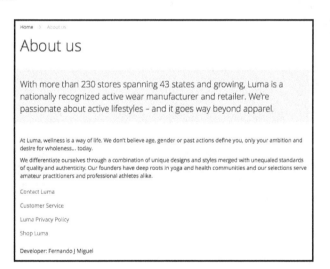

Good practices in Magento theming

There are a number of points that a good Magento 2 theme will typically abide by:

- Take advantage of Magento theme inheritance to develop new themes
- Follow the basic directory structure proposed
- Restrict any .phtml (Magento template files) to just those that have been changed for use with the custom theme

Adhering to these guidelines of Magento theming makes it easier to upgrade your Magento installation without making changes to your theme files.

Summary

You've now looked into how a Magento 2 theme works in theory including the terminology used in Magento themes, websites and stores scope, elements that make up a Magento theme, theme inheritance in Magento, good practice guidelines to consider when creating a custom Magento theme, Magento's Blank theme and its interaction with Luma theme and, at least but not last, custom Variables application.

In the next chapters, you will begin customizing Magento themes and look into Magento theming in more detail.

3
Magento 2 Theme Layout

*"Almost all quality improvement comes via simplification of design, manufacturing...
layout, processes, and procedures" – Tom Peters.*

Now that you've looked at what Magento has to offer in terms of themes, how themes in
Magento work, and the terminology you can use to describe the various aspects of Magento
themes, you can begin to look at customizing the look and feel of your store. In this chapter,
we'll cover the following topics:

- Magento 2 and Model-View-Controller architecture
- Command-Line Interface
- Magento 2 theme files
- Caching system
- Magento 2 layout system
- Creating your first Magento 2 theme
- Magento theme debug

Before developing your own Magento 2 theme, this chapter will explain some new
concepts, resources, and tools that will assist in theme development. You'll notice very soon
the importance of building a solid understanding of the Magento 2 theme infrastructure
when you start to professionally build your very own Magento 2 solutions.

Magento 2 and Model-View-Controller architecture

Magento 2 uses **Model-View-Controller** (**MVC**) as the software architectural pattern, which is responsible mainly for organizing the entire system's process structure at the coding level and establishing the means for the system to be flexible and extensible.

MVC distinguishes three layers of software activities, aiming for high cohesion and loosely coupling the modules responsible for the operation of Magento 2 systems. The three layers are described as follows:

- **Model**: The system modeling layer. Its main scope is handling system business rules and data persistence.
- **View**: This is responsible for the user information display layer, such as the product page and contact form.
- **Controller**: This is the layer that defines the main actions, requests, and responses of clients that may change the model's state and generate data views of the model layer.

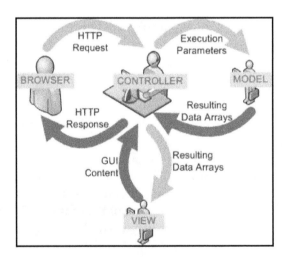

It's important to define these concepts so you can develop well. Even when dealing with a more technical matter (coding), it's highly recommended that you have these concepts well established. Of the three layers of the MVC architecture, Magento themes developers work mainly with the **View** layer.

Magento 2 Command-Line Interface

The Magento **Command-Line Interface** (**CLI**) seeks to automate processes and make life easier for developers to create unique solutions, serving as support for the execution of important procedures. The Magento 2 CLI tool can generate specific codes, perform deployment, change the status of the store, and even make backups by performing routines from the command line.

In previous versions of Magento, to disable the system cache, you would access the administrative area and change this option on the dashboard. With the Magento 2 CLI tool, it is possible perform this task with a simple command: `php bin/magento cache:disable`.

The Magento 2 CLI tool is available through the terminal (Unix-based) or command prompt (Windows) in the root directory of your Magento installation 2. You simply go to your root directory via the terminal or prompt and type the command `php bin/magento list`:

```
● ● ●                     packt — -bash — 80×38
[SunnyGo:packt fjmiguel$ php bin/magento list
Magento CLI version 2.0.0

Usage:
 command [options] [arguments]

Options:
 --help (-h)            Display this help message
 --quiet (-q)           Do not output any message
 --verbose (-v|vv|vvv)  Increase the verbosity of messages: 1 for normal output,
2 for more verbose output and 3 for debug
 --version (-V)         Display this application version
 --ansi                 Force ANSI output
 --no-ansi              Disable ANSI output
 --no-interaction (-n)  Do not ask any interactive question
```

Remember that the environment variable for PHP must be properly configured according to the XAMPP installation or any other environment to which you choose to work. See more at `http://php.net/manual/en/install.php`.

The php bin/magento list command displays a list of all the possible commands for use with the Magento 2 CLI tool. The commands are illustrated in the following table:

Main	
Command	**Function**
help	Displays help about a command
list	Lists commands

admin	
Command	**Function**
admin:user:create	Creates an administrator
admin:user:unlock	Unlocks the admin account

cache	
Command	**Function**
cache:clean	Cleans cache type(s)
cache:disable	Disables cache type(s)
cache:enable	Enables cache type(s)
cache:flush	Flushes cache storage used by cache type(s)
cache:status	Checks cache status

cron	
Command	**Function**
`cron:run`	Runs jobs by schedule

customer	
Command	**Function**
`customer:hash:upgrade`	Upgrade customer's hash according to the latest algorithm

deploy	
Command	**Function**
`deploy:mode:set`	Set application mode
`deploy:mode:show`	Displays current application mode

dev	
Command	**Function**
`dev:source-theme:deploy`	Collects and publishes source files for theme
`dev:tests:run`	Runs tests
`dev:urn-catalog:generate`	Generates the catalog of URNs to `*.xsd` mappings for the IDE to highlight XML
`dev:xml:convert`	Converts XML files using XSL style sheets

i18n	
Command	**Function**
`i18n:collect-phrases`	Discovers phrases in the codebase
`i18n:pack`	Saves language package
`i18n:uninstall`	Uninstalls language packages

indexer	
Command	**Function**
`indexer:info`	Shows allowed indexers
`indexer:reindex`	Reindexes data
`indexer:set-mode`	Sets the index mode type
`indexer:show-mode`	Shows the index mode
`indexer:status`	Shows the status of an indexer

info	
Command	**Function**
`info:adminuri`	Displays the Magento Admin URI
`info:backups:list`	Prints a list of available backup files
`info:currency:list`	Displays the list of available currencies
`info:dependencies:show-framework`	Shows the number of dependencies on the Magento framework
`info:dependencies:show-modules`	Shows the number of dependencies between modules
`info:dependencies:show-modules-circular`	Shows the number of circular dependencies between modules
`info:language:list`	Displays the list of available language locales
`info:timezone:list`	Displays the list of available timezones

maintenance	
Command	**Function**
`maintenance:allow-ips`	Sets maintenance mode exempt IPs
`maintenance:disable`	Disables maintenance mode
`maintenance:enable`	Enables maintenance mode
`maintenance:status`	Displays maintenance mode status

module	
Command	**Function**
`module:disable`	Disables specified modules
`module:enable`	Enables specified modules
`module:status`	Displays status of modules
`module:uninstall`	Uninstalls modules installed by composer

sampledata	
Command	**Function**
`sampledata:deploy`	Deploys sample data modules
`sampledata:remove`	Removes all sample data packages from `composer.json`
`sampledata:reset`	Resets all sample data modules for re-installation

setup	
Command	**Function**
`setup:backup`	Takes a backup of the Magento application code base, media, and database
`setup:config:set`	Creates or modifies the deployment configuration
`setup:cron:run`	Runs a cron job scheduled for setup application
`setup:db-data:upgrade`	Installs and upgrades data in the database
`setup:db-schema:upgrade`	Installs and upgrades the database schema
`setup:DB:status`	Checks if the database schema or data requires upgrade
`setup:di:compile`	Generates DI configuration and all non-existing interceptors and factories
`setup:di:compile-multi-tenant`	Generates all non-existing proxies and factories, and pre-compiles class definitions, inheritance information, and plugin definitions
`setup:install`	Installs the Magento application
`setup:performance:generate-fixtures`	Generates fixtures
`setup:rollback`	Rolls back the Magento application codebase, media, and database
`setup:static-content:deploy`	Deploys static view files
`setup:store-config:set`	Installs the store configuration
`setup:uninstall`	Uninstalls the Magento application
`setup:upgrade`	Upgrades the Magento application, database data, and schema

theme	
Command	**Function**
`theme:uninstall`	Uninstalls the theme

 Remember to use the `php bin/magento help` command to view which parameters can be used for a particular command. See more at `http://de vdocs.magento.com/guides/v2.0/config-guide/cli/config-cli.htm l`.

Magento 2 theme files

Magento 2 works with two groups of view files:

- **Static view files**: These are composed of images, JavaScript, and CSS files that do not undergo any processing at the server level
- **Dynamic view files**: These files are processed by the server, such as `.less`, templates and layouts files.

If you have no knowledge of **LESS** files, do not worry. In the next chapter, chapter 4, *Magento UI Library*, we will address this issue.

These two groups of files are linked directly to the cache management of Magento 2, as you will see in next topic.

Magento 2 cache system

The Magento cache system has evolved since previous versions. In addition to greater power, it can be completely managed by the Magento 2 CLI tool. The Magento cache system manages the following types of cache:

- **Config**: Contains all the settings of stored modules
- **Layout**: Contains the build page layouts
- **HTML Block**: Contains the compilation of HTML fragments (blocks)
- **Collections Date**: Stores database queries
- **Data Definition Language**: Stores information about the database schema

- **Entity attributes value (EAV)**: Contains metadata values defined in your Magento 2 admin panel, for example, name, price, and sku
- **Page cache**: Generates caching of all HTML pages rendered by Magento 2
- **Reflection**: Removes the dependency of the WebAPI module of the Customer module
- **Translations**: Generates caching for all system translation files
- **Integration Configuration**: Compiles the integration system
- **Integration API Configuration**: Compiles integrations between APIs
- **Web Services Configuration**: Contains all the reference settings to the web service system

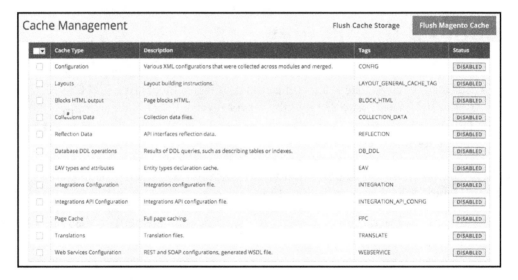

All of this parallel management in Magento 2's caching system allows the system, despite its robustness, to produce an optimum response time and performance for a production environment.

Magento 2 layout system

As seen in the previous chapter, the Magento 2 layout layer has a basic standard of positioning elements. If we think of a simple page that displays products in a given category, we have the following positioning vision:

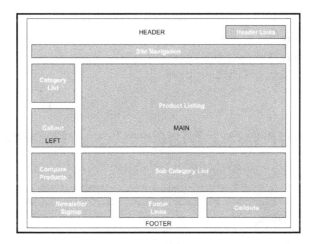

You can see that each element's position has a specific role in rendering the layout. The controller specifies the rendering of each block according to their respective models and visualization layers:

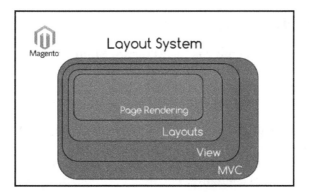

The Magento 2 layout system, defined by XML files, is responsible for manipulating elements and the behavior of each block or page to be rendered by creating parameters to feed the system. It is correct that the layout files influence the behavior and performance of the **View** layer when the rendering happens.

The layout layer is divided into the following sections:

- **Page layout**: This is responsible for declaring the general structure of the page, for example, a three-column layout. It operates mainly within the `<body>` element at the time of page rendering.
- **Page configuration**: This is responsible for reporting meta information, content types, and structure information. It operates mainly within the `<html>`, `<head>`, and `<body>` elements at the time of page rendering.
- **Generic layout**: This has the same powers as page configuration but is used for AJAX requests and HTML snippets.

Creating your first Magento 2 theme

After learning some of the basic concepts of the structure that accompanies the creation of Magento themes, it's time to work on creating your first simple Magento theme. Before creating the theme, it's necessary to explain to you, dear reader, a few important concepts of Magento theme development.

This step is very important for defining a standard process of developing themes, which will involve support tools, coding, and implementation for the visualization of the final result.

Magento Modes

One of the new features of Magento 2 is the **Magento Mode** feature. With this feature, you can choose how the system will behave with server requests.

Magento modes are divided into three options:

- **Default mode**: This is the way that Magento 2 operates normally. One of the characteristics is that errors are never shown to the user, and the static files are cached. This mode is ideal if the Magento system works on only one server without the settings changing. The default mode, however, is not optimized for a production environment.
- **Production mode**: This is ideal for deployment in a production environment. Errors and exceptions are not shown to the user and static files are generated in the cache system, prioritizing system performance.

- **Developer mode**: In this mode, static files are not cached, and system errors and exceptions are displayed to users. In this mode, there is no need to manage the external Internet traffic.

For development purposes, developer mode will be used once the proposed environment is running locally. To activate developer mode, follow these steps:

1. Open a terminal or command prompt.
2. Go to the root folder of your Magento installation.
3. Run the php bin/magento deploy:mode:set developer command.

Take a look at the following screenshot:

After this adjustment, it is necessary to give written permission again in the var directory.

> For more information, go to http://devdocs.magento.com/guides/v2.0 /config-guide/bootstrap/magento-modes.html.

Disabling Magento's cache

The preparations for the development of your first theme are almost done! Once Magento has been set up to operate in developer mode, you need to disable the caching system so that you can develop real-time solutions.

Before disabling the caching system, it is interesting to check the current status of your Magento 2 cache system. To do this, follow these steps:

1. Open a terminal or command prompt.
2. Go to the root folder of your Magento 2 installation.
3. Run the php bin/magento cache:status command.

Take a look at the following screenshot:

```
[SunnyGo:packt fjmiguel$ php bin/magento cache:status
Current status:
                        config: 1
                        layout: 1
                    block_html: 1
                   collections: 1
                    reflection: 1
                        db_ddl: 1
                           eav: 1
            config_integration: 1
        config_integration_api: 1
                     full_page: 1
                     translate: 1
             config_webservice: 1
SunnyGo:packt fjmiguel$
```

By default, all the caching systems appear activated with the value 1. To disable the caching system, just follow the previous steps, but now you need run the `php bin/magento cache:disable` command as shown in the following screenshot:

```
[SunnyGo:packt fjmiguel$ php bin/magento cache:disable
Changed cache status:
                        config: 1 -> 0
                        layout: 1 -> 0
                    block_html: 1 -> 0
                   collections: 1 -> 0
                    reflection: 1 -> 0
                        db_ddl: 1 -> 0
                           eav: 1 -> 0
            config_integration: 1 -> 0
        config_integration_api: 1 -> 0
                     full_page: 1 -> 0
                     translate: 1 -> 0
             config_webservice: 1 -> 0
SunnyGo:packt fjmiguel$
```

All Magento 2 caching systems have been disabled, as can be seen in the preceding screenshot.

Theme development

To start the development of your first theme, it is necessary to have a text/code editor. One good option is **Atom** (`https://atom.io/`), but you, dear reader, can use the editor of your preference.

Once you have the editor ready to use, create the `htdocs/Packt/app/design/frontend/Packt` directory. This directory will be the `vendor` directory of your theme. With this root `vendor`, we can extend and create multiple themes with small distinctions within the same `Vendor`.

Create the `htdocs/Packt/app/design/frontend/Packt/helloworld` directory. This directory represents the `theme` directory to be created. Now follow these instructions:

1. Open your favorite code editor.
2. Create a new file called `theme.xml` within `app/design/frontend/design/Packt/helloworld`.
3. Enter the following code `theme.xml` the file:

```
<theme xmlns:xsi="http://www.w3.org/2001/XMLSchema-
instance"xsi:noNamespaceSchemaLocation="urn:magento:framework:
Config/etc/theme.xsd">
<title>Hello World theme</title>
<parent>Magento/blank</parent>
<!-- <media>
<preview_image>media/preview.jpg</preview_image>
</media>--></theme>
```

It's a basic declaration for the Magento system to recognize our theme as an official theme. This code configures the theme name, parent, and preview image. The preview image is a preview for basic visualization purposes. We don't have a preview image at the moment; that's why the code is commented, to avoid unnecessary errors.

Once we have the basic configurations, we need to register the theme in Magento:

1. Open your preferred code editor.
2. Create new file named `registration.php` in your theme directory, `app/design/frontend/Packt/helloworld/registration.php`.
3. Use the following code in `registration.php` and save the file:

```php
<?php
\Magento\Framework\Component\ComponentRegistrar::register(
\Magento\Framework\Component\ComponentRegistrar::THEME,
'frontend/Packt/helloworld', __DIR__);
```

This code simply registers our theme in Magento by passing a parameter of your new theme's structure directory.

Creating the static files directories

The static files will be stored in the web directory. Inside the web directory, you will organize the static files according to their scope. Create a new directory called web in your theme directory, `app/design/frontend/Packt/helloworld/web`, and create the following directory structure:

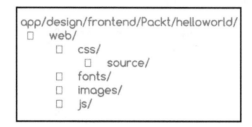

With this simple structure, you can manage all the static files of your custom theme.

Creating a theme logo

By default, in Magento 2 the theme logo is always recognized by the system with the name `logo.svg`. The Magento 2 also recognizes the logo's default directory as `<theme_dir>/web/images/logo.svg`. So, if you have a `logo.svg` file, you simply put the file in the right directory.

But if you want to work with a different logo name with a different format, you have to declare it in Magento by using the layout files declaration. We will make a declaration for this new logo in the `Magento_Theme` directory, because the new logo overrides the `Magento_Theme` module.

We will override this module by taking advantage of the fallback system. As you may have noticed, Magento has a specific pattern of declaring elements. It's the way that Magento organize its life cycle.

Let's declare a new theme logo:

1. Choose one logo for the example and save the file as `logo.png` in `app/design/frontend/Packt/helloworld/Magento_Theme/web/images` directory.
2. Move your new `logo.png` image to the `images` directory.
3. Open your preferred code editor.
4. Create new file named `default.xml` in your `layout` directory: `app/design/frontend/Packt/helloworld/Magento_Theme/layout`.
5. Place the following code in `default.xml` and save the file:

```
    <page xmlns:xsi="http://www.w3.org/2001/XMLSchema-instance"
xsi:noNamespaceSchemaLocation="urn:magento:framework:View/Layout/etc/page_c
onfigu        ration.xsd">
        <body>
        <referenceBlock name="logo">
        <arguments>
        <argument name="logo_file"
xsi:type="string">Magento_Theme/images/logo.png</argument>
        <argument name="logo_img_width" xsi:type="number">200</argument>
        <argument name="logo_img_height" xsi:type="number">150</argument>
        </arguments>
        </referenceBlock>
        </body>
        </page>
```

This declaration has three different arguments to manage the following attributes of your new logo: filename, width, and height. Don't forget to replace the `your_logo_width` and `your_logo_height` attributes with the correct size of the logo that you choose.

The `logo_file` argument seems to be wrong because we created our image in the `Magento_Theme/web/images` directory, but thank god this is not true. I'll explain: when we activate the new theme, Magento processes the static files and copies the static files to the `pub/static` directory. This occurs because the static files can be cached by Magento and the correct directory for this is the `pub` directory. So, we need to create the `web` directory so Magento recognize the files as static files.

The final Theme directory structure is illustrated as follows:

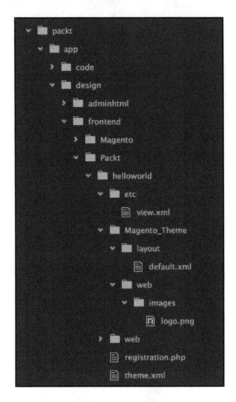

Applying the theme

Once we have the theme ready to launch, we need to activate it in the Magento admin dashboard. The steps are as follows:

1. Access the Magento admin area (`http://localhost/packt/admin_packt`) in your favorite browser.
2. Navigate to **Stores** | **Configuration** | **Design**.
3. Select the **Hello World theme** option as your **Design Theme** and save the configuration.

Take a look at the following screenshot:

Navigate to the home page of your site by accessing `http://localhost/packt` to see the final result:

Magento 2 theme debug

From now on, you will work more effectively with Magento 2 theme development. You received enough information so you can start developing your own Magento 2 theme.

Before moving on to the next topics, I would like to end this chapter with a presentation of the Magento debug tool.

With this tool, you can monitor the page rendering behavior of Magento 2, and thereby create a more effective environment for layout changes that you apply in your future projects.

To enable this feature, follow these instructions:

1. Access the Magento admin area (`http://localhost/packt/admin_packt`) in your favorite browser.
2. Navigate to **Stores** | **Configuration** | **Advanced** | **Developer**.
3. Change the **Enabled Template Path Hints for Storefront** option to **Yes** and save the changes.

Take a look at the following screenshot:

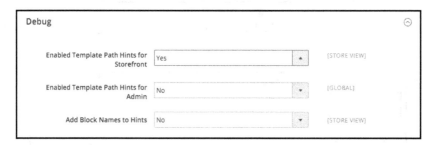

You can set **YES** for **Add Block Names to Hints** if you want. This option shows the block names in the frontend, easing your identification of blocks that are used in Magento.

Go to the homepage (`http://localhost/packt`) to see the location system of templates:

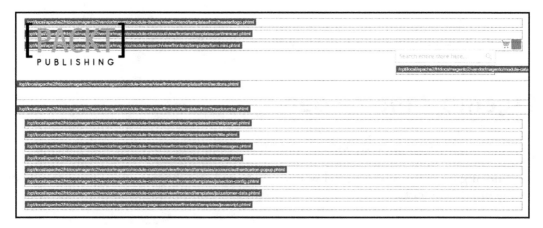

With the display of the path of each module being rendered on the page, you can plan your development more effectively by keeping in mind what kinds of change and what modules you need to improve or maintain. You can always change this status to the previous configuration if you want.

Summary

In this chapter, you began to look into customizing your Magento store with content, including the following:

- Concepts surrounding the Magento MVC architecture
- Contextualizing the view layer of MVC and how it will be applied
- An overview of Magento's cache, and a guide to how to disable it
- The layout system and how it works
- How to change your store's logo
- The basic procedure of creating your theme
- Tools and resources to support theme development

In the next chapter, you will study one of the most important Magento 2 native resources for theme development: the Magento UI library. You will find out how the application of the UI library can enrich your projects.

4
Magento UI Library

"The more users' expectations prove right, the more they will feel in control of the system and the more they will like it." – Jakob Nielson – Ph.D. in human-computer interaction from the Technical University of Denmark in Copenhagen

The evolution of the Magento system brought significant change to the way developers work to create unique and customized solutions in Magento 2. The absorption of technologies that could leverage this evolution of the Magento system was a watershed, for the system could achieve an even higher status in the Magento community of enthusiasts, developers, and system administrators.

In this chapter, we will look at one of the technologies that have totally changed the way the development of themes for Magento 2 is understood: The Magento User Interface Library.

The following topics will be covered in this chapter:

- Magento 2 UI
- LESS and CSS preprocessing
- LESS compilation in Magento 2
- Magento 2 UI library
- Testing Magento 2 UI library

Magento 2 UI

The **User Interface** (**UI**) has been the subject of great relevance to applications, websites, and software that aim to deliver simple, easy to use content to users.

According to the **Usability.gov** website (http://www.usability.gov), the leading resource for user design (UX) best practices and guidelines (favored among practitioners and students in both government and private sectors), an ideal UI focuses on anticipating what users might need to do, and ensures that the interface has elements that are easy to access, understand, and use in order to facilitate those actions:

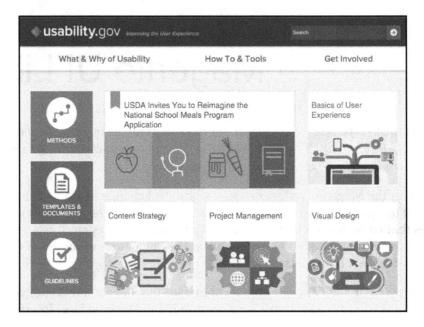

As can be seen in previous chapters, one of the major changes between Magento 1 and Magento 2 was the adoption and improvement of technologies in order to generate better results, such as the following:

- Better performance
- Support for different devices
- Maintainability
- Scalability

According to these premises, and following this book's scope, the system performance has better results when using techniques and technologies that reduce the rendering time of the visual elements of the page. Thus, the following technologies were adopted by the Magento 2 development team:

- HTML5 + CSS3 + LESS (CSS preprocessor)
- **Responsive Web Design (RWD)** default theme

- Magento UI library
- Built-in PHP LESS Compiler
- **Web Content Accessibility Guidelines (WCAG)** 2.0 compliant

Take a look at the following diagram:

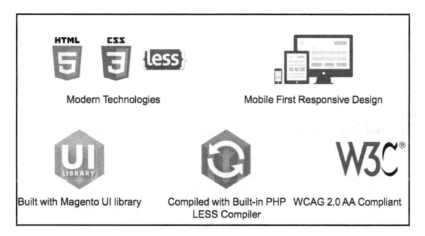

Image credits: http://goo.gl/whZ5YL

See more about the new features of the Magento 2 frontend development, available on the official presentation at http://goo.gl/whZ5YL.

LESS and CSS preprocessing

One of the major questions that is always raised when developers work with large and complex projects that require many frontend rules via CSS, is: how will I work my code in a sustainable, scalable, and modular way?

The preprocessing in CSS, although not a silver bullet for all issues, promotes the writing of reusable and maintainable CSS codes, increasing productivity and reducing the amount of coding in the project, thereby achieving a better performance.

In Magento 1.9, the solution used for CSS compilation was the **SASS (Syntactically Awesome Style Sheets)** technology (`http://sass-lang.com/`). The SASS is a CSS extension that implements additional features for use in their projects, such as variables, mixins, inline imports, and so on. For Magento 2, there is a project that still uses the SASS technology, and this project is maintained on GitHub at `https://github.com/SnowdogApp s/magento2-theme-blank-sass`.

In order to follow the natural evolution of CSS technology by using the best management techniques, the Magento development team has adopted **LESS** technology (`http://www.le sscss.org/`) for Magento 2, as a CSS preprocessing solution.

LESS extends the natural features of CSS and absorbs all the main features of a CSS preprocessor, which provides all the advantages discussed earlier. LESS was created in 2009 by Alexis Sellier, and began to be portable to different programming languages in 2012 through the contribution of design enthusiasts and developers.

Now that you understand the context of this subject, you can see, in the coming examples, just how powerful the LESS preprocessor can be by creating a modular code and providing a highly scalable system. The following examples will serve only as a reference for the tests that you will do in Magento 2. However, feel free to practice them separately by consulting the quick-start guide of LESS, available at `http://www.lesscss.org/#using-less`. Take a look at the following image:

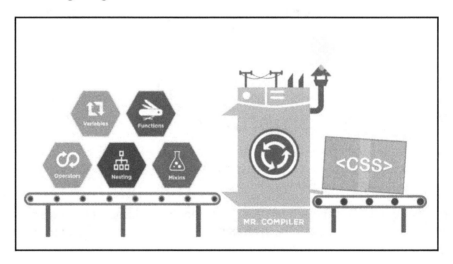

Image credits: `http://www.slideshare.net/sunbash1/sass-vsless`

Custom variables

Let's say you were writing a CSS code to determine the font size of the `div` tag. You would probably use the following code:

```
div{
    font-size: 12px;
}
```

At this point, you would probably use custom variables for CSS preprocessing. By using custom variables, you can plan and parameterize your CSS code effectively:

```
@myContentFont: 12px;

div {
    font-size: @myContentFont;
}
```

Every time you need a change in font size, just change the default variable so that your page's rendering behavior can be disseminated within your frontend development project.

Functions

The LESS preprocessor has some functions to use in your code. The `darken` function, for example, decreases the lightness of a color:

```
@myColor: #00FF00;
.box .myBox {
    background-color: @myColor;
    border: 3px solid darken(@myColor, 20%);
}
```

In the previous example, you can vary the tone of the same color using the `darken` function.

 For more information about the LESS functions, please visit the official documentation, available at `http://www.lesscss.org/functions/`.

Mixins

The **Mixins** feature is very similar to functions in programming languages. The idea of using Mixins is to make a reusable code through declared classes on the LESS preprocessor. Here's how it works:

```
.packt, #magento {
  color: red;
}
.mixin-class {
  .packt();
}
.mixin-id {
  #magento();
}
```

The `.mixin-class` and `.mixin-id` classes reuse the `#magento` `.packt` class through the `.packt()` and `#magento()` mixins call. This call passes to the LESS compiler, which returns the processed CSS:

```
.packt, #magento {
  color: red;
}
.mixin-class {
  color: red;
}
.mixin-id {
  color: red;
}
```

So, you can make use of this feature to reuse previously developed classes in your project to gain performance and reduce the implementation time.

> For more information, visit the official documentation for LESS, available at `http://www.lesscss.org/features/#mixins-feature`.

Operators

LESS provides arithmetic and logical operators for the creation of special rules that you want to implement in your code. This can be very helpful when the developer wants to implement, for example, a rule for responsive design.

Here's an example of LESS arithmetic operators implementing some special rules:

```less
@myFontSize: 12px;

div {
    font-size: @myFontSize;
}

div .double{
  font-size: @myFontSize * 2;
}
Here is the result after the compilation:
div {
    font-size: 12px;
}
div .double {
  font-size: 24px;
}
```

Very simple to use, isn't it? Now let's look at an example using logical operators:

```less
.mixin (@a) when (lightness(@a) >= 50%) {
  background-color: black;
}
.mixin (@a) when (lightness(@a) < 50%) {
  background-color: white;
}

.mixin (@a) { color: @a; }
```

In the previous example, two functions are created that have a specific behavior according to the parameter passed, according to the logic check implemented with the word when, and with the help of the lightness function, which extracts the brightness of a particular color by returning a percentage value.

Once the mixin rules were defined, the LESS preprocessor calls are performed as follows:

```less
.packtPub { .mixin(#ddd) }
.magento { .mixin(#555) }
```

In practice, through the parameter passed to the mixin function, the LESS preprocessor will check if the last color has lower or higher indices of brightness and will respond to the client/user with the following processed CSS:

```less
.packtPub {
  background-color: black;
  color: #ddd;
```

```
}
.magento {
  background-color: white;
  color: #555;
}
```

See that the `mixin` makes the checking, the logic validation, and a merge of code through a single call for the parameterized class.

Nestings

The **nestings** feature allows for greater readability and organization of the code being implemented, as can be seen in the following example:

```
@myLinkColor: #ffff00;
@myLinkHover: #ffffff;

ul {
    margin: 0;

    li {
        float: left;
    }

    a {
        color: @myLinkColor;

        &:hover {
            color: @myLinkHover;
        }
    }
}
```

The main idea of the nestings feature, technically speaking, is to group all CSS rules within the scope of tags that are being affected with the developed CSS. Sound complicated? Look at the processed CSS output of the previous example:

```
ul { margin: 0; }
ul li { float: left; }
ul a { color: #ffff00; }
ul a:hover { color: #ffffff; }
```

LESS compilation in Magento 2

Magento 2 provides two compile options for the LESS technology:

- **Server-Side compilation LESS**: This is the default compilation model used by the Magento 2 system, and is performed by the server using the LESS `PHP` library. It is suitable for production environments.
- **Client-Side compilation LESS**: This is the compilation made by the client machine via the browser using the native `less.js` library. It is suitable for non-production environments.

In the Magento admin panel, you can adjust this setting by following this recipe:

1. In Magento Admin, navigate to **Stores** | **Configuration** | **ADVANCED** | **Developer**.
2. In the **Store** view, select **Default Config**.
3. Under **Front-end development workflow**, select the compilation mode: **Server side less compilation** or **Client side less compilation**.
4. Click **Save Config**.

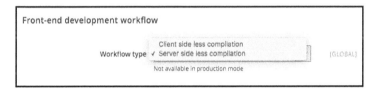

The Magento UI library

The Magento UI library was created so that the developers of Magento themes could use a ready and optimized solution that supported the development of new Magento themes. The library is based on the LESS preprocessor, which facilitates the implementation of customizations in Magento 2 theme development.

The Magento UI library provides the following elements and properties so that theme developers can customize the user interface of their projects:

- **actions-toolbar**: Includes a set of actions on a page, such as submit buttons and links to navigate the page
- **breadcrumbs**: Allows users to keep track of their location within the website

- **buttons**: A set of different buttons to use in your project
- **dropdowns**: A set of drop-downs to use in your project
- **forms**: Customize your forms using the mixins and by configuring the global variables
- **icons**: Can be added to any HTML tag, and represented by fonts, images, or sprites
- **layout**: Provides mixins for flexible page layout customization
- **loaders**: Provides an animation while the page is loading
- **messages**: Provides four types of messages: Info, warning, error, and success
- **pagination**: Display numbers of the page
- **popups**: Implements a popup to use in your project
- **ratings**: Uses font icons as rate symbols
- **sections**: Uses tabs and accordions to separate the content in sections
- **tables**: Provides customization options for the tables cells
- **tooltips**: Provides four tooltips types: Top, bottom, left, and right
- **typography**: Provides mixins for typography styling
- **global variables**: You can consult the list of global variables to use in your project

In the following example, available in the Magento 2 official documentation (`http://goo.g l/nydsch`), you can see the layers in which the UI elements act in order to render the product page:

At first, it may be difficult to see that CSS preprocessing was used to render the product page. Let's strengthen this concept in a more practical way by focusing on the **breadcrumbs** element.

The Magento UI library is located in the directory `<magento_root>/lib/web/css/source/lib`, as illustrated in the following screenshot:

It is possible to see a file called `breadcrumb.less`. Open this file in your favorite code editor to see the content.

Looking at the code, you will notice the important concepts of LESS used to create preprocessing rules for the breadcrumbs element, as shown in the following code snippet:

```less
& when (@_breadcrumbs-icon-use = true) {  // Use font icon as a separating symbol
    .item:not(:last-child) {
        .lib-icon-font(
            @_icon-font-content: @_breadcrumbs-icon-font-content,
            @_icon-font: @_icon-font,
            @_icon-font-size: @_icon-font-size,
            @_icon-font-line-height: @_icon-font-line-height,
            @_icon-font-color: @_icon-font-color,
            @_icon-font-margin: @_icon-font-margin,
            @_icon-font-vertical-align: @_icon-font-vertical-align,
            @_icon-font-position: after
        );
    }
}
```

Notice the application of LESS concepts, namely logical operator, custom variables, and nestings.

Now, open the `_breadcrumb.less` file, available in the `<magento_root>/vendor/magento/theme-frontend-blank/web/css/source` directory:

```less
// /**
//  * Copyright © 2015 Magento. All rights reserved.
//  * See COPYING.txt for license details.
//  */

//
// Common
// _____

& when (@media-common = true) {
    .breadcrumbs {
        .lib-breadcrumbs();
    }
}
```

In addition to the concepts discussed earlier, the LESS file performs a mixin (similar to a `call` function) so that the breadcrumbs element of the Magento UI library can be used in the Magento Blank theme.

The degree of modularity that the Magento UI library brings to developers is now clear. You can reuse code by applying high cohesion and low coupling for the frontend system in order to customize and develop new Magento 2 themes.

Take a look at the following diagram:

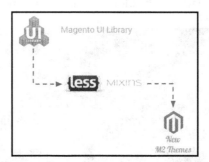

The official Magento UI library documentation is available at the Magento 2 official repository, available at `https://github.com/magento/magento2 /tree/2.0/lib/web/css/docs`.

Testing the Magento UI library

In the previous chapter, `Chapter 3`, *Magento 2 Theme Layout*, we created the **Hello World** theme, but without any change in the CSS structure. Now that you've gained the knowledge of the use of the Magento UI library in your projects, it will be far simpler to understand the flow processes and the application of techniques in developing Magento 2 themes. Let's make some customizations in our Hello World theme using the Magento UI library:

1. Copy the file `<magento_root>/vendor/magento/theme-frontend-blank/web/css/_styles.less` to `packt/app/design/frontend/Packt/compstore/web/css`.

2. Open the copied file and insert an `import` command, as shown in the following example:

```
@import 'source/lib/_lib.less';
@import 'source/_sources.less';
@import 'source/_components.less';
@import 'source/helloworld.less';
```

3. Save the file.

The `_styles.less` file, besides being used as a standard nomenclature within the Magento 2 development environment, is also responsible for loading the Magento UI library to your project. Note that in the last line of the LESS code we are making the import of a custom LESS file, which we will create in the sequence.

Now, open your favorite code editor, create the file `helloworld.less` under the directory `<magento_root>/app/design/frontend/helloworld/web/css/source`, and type following code:

```
@color-compstore: #000;

body{
   background: @color-compstore;
}
```

This file will be responsible for customizations that you want to implement in your new Magento 2 theme project.

Now, here comes a very important point: The Magento UI library works with predefined custom variables. You can and should view them in the standard LESS library directory to understand them better. Despite the custom variables predefinition, the theme developers can override them by creating the `_theme.less` file. So every variable that is rewritten in this file will be used throughout the Magento UI library on your theme, and there is no need to write new, complex CSS rules. Much easier isn't it?

Let's create the `_theme.less` file by following this recipe:

1. Create the `_theme.less` file under the directory `packt/app/design/frontend/compstore/web/css/source`.

2. Type the following code:

   ```
   //Change navigation background color
   @navigation__background: @color-white;
   //Change the link color
   @link__color: @color-white;
   ```

3. Save the file.

> For more information about the `_theme.less` file, visit the official documentation at `http://devdocs.magento.com/guides/v2.0/frontend -dev-guide/themes/theme-structure.html`.

Now `helloworld.less` and `_theme.less`, the website background, the navigation background, and the link colors have changed according to the new variables of the Hello World theme.

Sometimes when you make changes in the Magento 2 structure or activate a new theme, you need to deploy the theme and module changes. If you want to deploy your changes, follow these steps:

1. Open the terminal or Command Prompt.
2. Delete the directory `<magento_root>/pub/static/frontend/<Vendor>/<theme>/<locale>`.
3. Delete the directory `var/cache` (if enabled).
4. Delete the directory `var/view_preprocessed`.
5. Access the directory `<magento_root>/bin`.
6. Run the command `php magento setup:static-content:deploy`.

In some cases, it is necessary to give written permission to the directories again.

Let's see the final result:

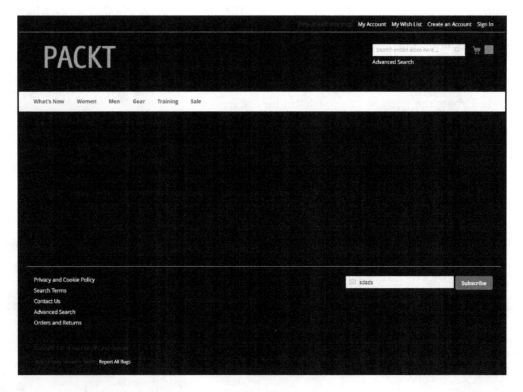

Strengthening the concepts, you realize that it was created as an extension of the Magento UI library through the `helloworld.less` and `_theme.less` files by adding specific items to test our theme project, demonstrating the flexibility, modularity, and scalability of the concept of preprocessing LESS implemented in the Magento 2 system.

 The Magento UI library documentation is available locally on your Magento installation through this link `http: //<magento_root>/pub/static/frontend/Magento/blank/en_US/css/docs/index.html`.

Summary

In this chapter, you have learned how the Magento UI library works, in addition to its main concepts and process flows. You also learned how to apply these concepts to develop new Magento 2 themes. With a well-founded understanding of the theory, you can deliver projects with higher quality and reliability.

In the test performed with the theme Hello World, using the Magento UI library, you applied the knowledge that you acquired and strengthened your understanding of the theoretical concepts.

In the next chapter, we will create a new theme by applying the concepts of Magento UI library. See you!

5
Creating a Responsive Magento 2 Theme

"I do not think there is any thrill that can go through the human heart like that felt by the inventor as he sees some creation of the brain unfolding to success... such emotions make a man forget food, sleep, friends, love, everything"
– Nikola Tesla

The previous chapters introduced various aspects, variables, and techniques that are part of the development of themes for Magento 2. It's important to note that the more you deepen your searches and participate in solutions development discussion groups, the faster you will develop a methodology to create your own schema to develop themes for Magento 2. This chapter's main mission is the practical application of concepts we've previously seen, by creating a new theme project called **BookStore**.

The following topics will be covered:

- Introducing the BookStore theme project
- Managing dependencies with Composer
- Building the BookStore theme
- Developing Magento 2 templates

The BookStore theme project

The BookStore theme is a Magento 2 practical theme project that introduces to you, dear reader, the basics of a professional approach of Magento's theme development.

Commercially, the development of Magento themes has opened an interesting market for developers through specialized marketplaces, such as the **Forest** theme (`http://www.theme forest.net`). I strongly suggest you take a look at the **Become an Author** page (`http://www .themeforest.net/become_an_author`) in order to explore the options to monetize your Magento theme development expertise. Logically, you have to work harder before you can publish and sell your own theme solution, but it will be worth it!

Managing dependencies with Composer

Magento works with **Composer** (`https://www.getcomposer.org`) to generate reliable deployments of Magento components. Composer is a dependency manager for PHP created by Nils Adermann and Jordi Boggiano. This is a great evolution in the Magento system because this management can provide a powerful environment for modules and theme management.

Inspired by **npm** (`https://www.npmjs.com`) and **bundler** (`http://www.bundler.io`), Composer manages the dependencies of your project and installs packages using the `composer.json` file in the Magento module or theme. This kind of management is very useful once each library has your specific dependency. Composer doesn't let you waste your time by connecting the dependencies of every deployment you want to perform.

In this chapter, you will declare the `composer.json` file, containing important information about your new theme. However, I suggest you delve more into dependency management in order to enrich your professional background.

Installing Composer on Unix-like operating systems

To install Composer on Unix-like OSes (Unix, Linux, OSX), you simply run these two commands from a terminal:

```
$ curl -s https://getcomposer.org/installer | php
$ sudo mv composer.phar /usr/local/bin/composer
```

The first command downloads the installation file, `composer.phar`. The second command moves the file to the `bin` directory in order to install Composer globally on your computer.

Run the following command to check whether Composer was successfully installed:

```
$ composer
```

The `composer` command lists all available Composer commands and descriptions:

Installing Composer on Windows

To install Composer on Windows, you simply have to download and execute `Composer-Setup.exe`, available at `https://getcomposer.org/Composer-Setup.exe`.

This executable file will install the latest Composer version and set up your `PATH` variable to use the `composer` command in Command Prompt. Open Command Prompt and run the `composer` command to get the list of available commands and test Composer.

Building the BookStore theme

Magento 2 can handle different themes inside the same vendor scope, as you saw in the earlier chapters. We have created the Hello World theme inside Packt's vendor, but with reduced options inside the theme. The idea behinds the Hello World theme was to introduce to you some basic concepts. Now it's time to move up to the next level! The theme project proposal of this chapter is called BookStore.

First of all, you have to build the theme directory in
`<magento_root>/app/design/frontend/Packt/bookstore`:

Clarifications about the theme's directory structure:

- `etc`: This usually handles the XML configuration of some components
- `Magento_Theme`: This overrides the native `Magento_Theme` module by adding new functionalities
- `media`: This stores the preview image of the BookStore theme
- `web`: This handles created CSS and images files

It is time to create the `theme.xml` file in the
`<magento_root>/app/design/frontend/Packt/bookstore` directory with the following code:

```
<theme xmlns:xsi="http://www.w3.org/2001/XMLSchema-instance"
xsi:noNamespaceSchemaLocation="urn:magento:framework:Config/etc/theme.xsd">
    <title>BookStore | Building Knowledge</title>
    <parent>Magento/luma</parent>
    <media>
        <preview_image>media/preview.jpg</preview_image>
    </media>
</theme>
```

The `theme.xml` file follows a specific pattern to be considered a valid XML file for the declaration of themes in Magento 2. First, the file creates a reference to the main tag `<theme></theme>`, which defines the attributes of the **XMLNS** (**XML namespace**), responsible for the W3C XML schema formalism, and contains the definition of the **XSI** (**XML instance**) that will be responsible for validating the schema of the **URN** (**uniform resource name**), which will reference the **XSD** (**XML schema definition**) file, called `theme.xsd`.

 To learn more about XMLNS, XSI, and XSD, refer to the official documentation, available at W3C `https://www.w3.org/TR/xmlschema-1` and to learn more about URN and XSD schema validation in Magento 2, refer to the official documentation, available at `http://devdocs.magento.com/guides/v2.0/extension-dev-guide/build/XSD-XML-validation.html`.

The main idea behind the declarations of these attributes is to organize, in a scalable and sustainable way, the declaration of Magento 2 themes as well as creating a standard mechanism for the validation of the theme declaration.

The other tags are easier to understand:

- `<title>`: This contains the main title of your theme
- `<parent>`: This contains the theme being inherited (the parent theme of your new theme)
- `<media>`: This contains media information used in your theme, for example, the theme preview image.

Create a preview image of the theme 800×800 pixels large, and save it in the `Packt/bookstore/media` directory. At this point, you can select any image to preview as a placeholder, for example, the Magento logo centered in an 800×800-pixel image.

The next step is create the `registration.php` file in the `<magento_root>/app/design/frontend/Packt/bookstore` directory, with the following code in it:

```php
<?php

\Magento\Framework\Component\ComponentRegistrar::register(
    \Magento\Framework\Component\ComponentRegistrar::THEME,
    'frontend/Packt/bookstore',
    __DIR__
);
```

All Magento components, including modules, themes, and language packs, must be duly registered with the Magento system. The `ComponentRegistrar` class is the one that contains this task in the Magento 2 system.

Each component must have a `registration.php` file in your root directory. In the case of the BookStore theme statement, the `ComponentRegistrar` class is declaring the THEME attribute as a scope-resolution operator, which declares the register of the component as a Magento theme.

> To learn more about registering components in Magento 2, refer to the official documentation at `http://devdocs.magento.com/guides/v2.0/extension-dev-guide/build/component-registration.html` and to learn more about the scope-resolution operator, refer to the official PHP documentation at `http://php.net/manual/en/language.oop5.paamayim-nekudotayim.php`.

Let's now declare the `composer.json` file in the `Packt/bookstore` directory, with the following code in it:

```json
{
    "name": "packt/bookstore",
    "description": "BookStore theme",
    "require": {
        "php": "~5.5.0|~5.6.0|~7.0.0",
        "magento/theme-frontend-luma": "~100.0",
        "magento/framework": "~100.0"
    },
    "type": "magento2-theme",
    "version": "1.0.0",
    "license": [
        "OSL-3.0",
        "AFL-3.0"
    ],
    "autoload": {
        "files": [ "registration.php" ]
    }
}
```

The file is in the JSON (`http://www.json.org`) format and handles important information about the project and its dependencies. This kind of control is crucial because it results in better organization in your project.

The principal parameters of `composer.json` are as follows:

- `name`: The name of the component
- `description`: The description of the component
- `require`: The dependencies of the project (PHP version, Magento libraries, and so on)
- `type`: The type of component (theme, module, and so on)
- `version`: The version of the component
- `license`: The licenses applied on the component (Open Source License, Academic Free License, and so on)
- `autoload`: The files and classes that will be autoloaded on component activation

Applying new CSS to the BookStore theme

All the files with the `.less` extension that you will create in your theme are compiled by the LESS engine, which we saw in `Chapter 4`, *Magento UI Library*, which creates the processed CSS file. Practically, it works as follows:

- **Frontend HTML/CSS declaration (browser)**: The `<link rel="stylesheet" type="text/css" media="screen and (min-width: 768px)" href="http://localhost/packt/pub/static/frontend/Packt/hellowor ld/en_US/css/styles-l.css" />` tag represents the deployed CSS file of the Hello World theme
- **LESS files**: The `styles-l.css` file is created after the processing of modules and themes into LESS files. For example, the `helloworld.less` file composes the `styles-l.css` file.

The `styles-l.css` file has all the processed LESS files, including `helloworld.less`. If you open `styles-l.css` in your browser to view its code and search for the declaration that you made previously in `helloworld.less`, you will find it minified along with the other CSS. Take a look at the following screenshot:

```
http://localhost/packt/pub/static/frontend/Packt/helloworld/en_US/css/styles-l.css

0}.modal-popup .modal-header{padding-bottom: 1.2rem;padding-top: 3rem}.modal-popup .m
popup .modal-footer-actions{text-align: right}@media (max-width: 768px){.modal-popup.
inner-wrap{-webkit-transform: translateX(0);transform: translateX(0)}.modal-popup.mod
webkit-transform: translateX(100%);transform: translateX(100%);transition-duration: .
property: transform, visibility;transition-timing-function: ease-in-out;width: auto}.
none}}body{background: #000}.fotorama-video-container:after{background: url(../Magent
'';height: 100px;left: 0;margin: auto;position: absolute;right: 0;top: 12px;width: 10
!important}.fotorama-video-container.video-unplayed:hover img{opacity: 0.6}.fotorama-
thumb-icon:after{background: url(../Magento_ProductVideo/img/gallery-sprite.png) bott
absolute;right: 0;top: 10px;width: 49px}.product-video{height: 75%;left: 0;position:
iframe{height: 100%;left: 0;position: absolute;top: 0;width: 100%;z-index: 9999}@medi
(orientation: landscape){.product-video{height: 100%;width: 81%}}.fotorama__arr.hidde
auto}.fotorama__stage__shaft:focus .fotorama__stage__frame.fotorama__active:after{bot
absolute;right: 0;top: 12px;width: 100px}.block-wishlist-search .form-wishlist-search
```

Now that you have memorized the LESS preprocessing flow, it's time to focus on applying the CSS. You will take advantage of the default theme of Magento 2 to create the BookStore theme, which inherits the Luma theme, which in turn inherits the Blank theme:

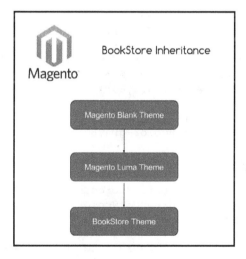

While planning, you can consider the functionalities already available in the other themes in order to apply your specific changes to the new theme. Keep in mind the techniques used in Chapter 4, *Magento UI Library*.

The ComponentRegistrar directory, under the Magento 2 root directory, handles all the native Magento modules and themes. The Magento Blank and Luma themes, which you have been working with until now, are available at vendor/magento/theme-frontend-blank and vendor/magento/theme-frontend-luma respectively.

The BookStore theme inherits all the features of these themes. It's important to fix these basic concepts to understand the context that you are inserted when you develop a Magento theme solution.

With a solid understanding of this behavior, let's create a custom CSS file for the BookStore theme:

1. Open your favorite code editor and create a file called _styles.less under the packt/app/design/frontend/Packt/bookstore/web/css directory.

2. Enter this code in the styles.less file:

```
@import 'source/lib/_lib.less';
@import 'source/_sources.less';
@import 'source/_components.less';
```

3. Save the file.

4. Change the theme color schema by creating the _theme.less file under the packt/app/design/frontend/bookstore/web/css/source directory:

```
//Changing the color structure
@bookstore-background: #ffffff;
@primary__color: @color-black;
@page__background-color: @bookstore-background;
@sidebar__background-color: @color-gray40;
@primary__color: @color-gray80;
@border-color__base: @color-gray76;
@link__color: @color-gray56;
@link__hover__color: @color-gray60;
//Buttons
@button__color: @color-gray20;
@button__background: @color-gray80;
@button__border: 1px solid @border-color__base;
@button-primary__background: @color-orange-red1;
@button-primary__border: 1px solid @color-orange-red2;
@button-primary__color: @color-white;
@button-primary__hover__background: darken(@color-orange-red1, 5%);
@button-primary__hover__border: 1px solid @color-orange-red2;
@button-primary__hover__color: @color-white;
//Navigation
@navigation__background: @color-gray82;
@navigation-desktop-level0-item__color: @color-black;
@navigation-desktop-level0-item__hover__color: @color-white;
@navigation-desktop-level0-item__active__color: @navigation-
desktop-level0-item__color;
//Miscelaneous
@tab-control__background-color: @page__background-color;
```

```
@form-element-input__background: @color-gray89;
@form-element-input-placeholder__color: @color-gray60;
@header-icons-color: @color-gray89;
@header-icons-color-hover: @color-gray60;
```

Set up the logo of the new theme to be responsive for mobile devices that access the BookStore theme. For this, create the `Magento_Theme/web/css/source` directory under the root directory of the BookStore theme, and copy to this directory the `file` `vendor/magento/theme-frontend-luma/Magento_Theme/web/css/source/_module.less`.

Open the file in your favorite code editor and, on line number 355 (approximately) edit the following code:

```
.media-width(@extremum, @break) when (@extremum = 'max') and (@break =
@screen__s) {
    .logo {
        margin-bottom: 13px;
        margin-top: 4px;
        margin: 0 0 @indent__s @indent__xl;
        max-width: 50%;
        position: relative;
        z-index: 5;
        img {
            display: block;
            max-height: 50%;
            max-width: 50%;
        }
    }
}
```

You will also make some changes in the product page. First, create the `Magento_Catalog/web/css/source` directory under the root directory of the BookStore theme, and copy to the new directory the file `vendor/magento/theme-frontend-luma/Magento_Catalog/web/css/source/_module.less`.

Open the file and edit as follows:

1. Around line number nine, change the variable value for `@product-info-price`, and insert a new variable:

   ```
   @product-default: @color-black;
   @product-info-price: @color-black;
   ```

2. Around line number 49, approximately, insert the attribute color for product name and price:

```
.price{
  color: @product-default;
}
  .product.name a {
     &:extend(.abs-product-link all);
     color: @product-default;
}
```

3. Around line number 152, approximately, insert the attribute color in the `.product-info-main` class:

```
.product-info-main {
color: @product-default;
```

4. Around line number 550, approximately, insert the new color for the page title:

```
.page-title{
     color: @product-default;
}
```

5. Around line number 625, approximately, change the sidebar font color:

```
.sidebar {
     color: @product-default;
```

Remember that the changes are only to be made in the previous code snippets. The remainder of the code should be unchanged.

Creating the BookStore logo

You can create a new logo for learning purposes using the **LogoMakr** free online service (`ht tp://www.logomakr.com`). It's a pretty easy tool for this particular purpose:

As an example, I've created this logo to apply on the new theme:

This educational graphic by Freepik (`http://www.freepik.com`) from Flaticon (`http://www .flaticon.com`) is licensed under Creative Commons BY 3.0. Made with Logo Maker.

After finishing the logo, create a new directory under `Magento_Theme` called `app/design/frontend/Packt/bookstore/Magento_Theme/web/images` and save the file as `logo.png`.

Feel free to use your own solution for logos instead of using Logo Maker.

Now, you have to set the new logo information in your theme, using the same process as in Chapter 3, *Magento 2 Theme Layout*. Create the new `default.xml` file under the `app/design/frontend/Packt/bookstore/Magento_Theme/layout` directory, with the following XML in it:

```
<page xmlns:xsi="http://www.w3.org/2001/XMLSchema-instance"
xsi:noNamespaceSchemaLocation="urn:magento:framework:View/Layout/etc/page_c
onfiguration.xsd">
    <body>
        <referenceBlock name="logo">
            <arguments>
                <argument name="logo_file"
xsi:type="string">Magento_Theme/images/logo.png</argument>
                <argument name="logo_img_width"
xsi:type="number">your_logo_width</argument>
<argument name="logo_img_height" xsi:type="number">your_logo_height
</argument>
            </arguments>
        </referenceBlock>
    </body>
</page>
```

Changing your store's design

It's time to activate the new theme like you learned in Chapter 3, *Magento 2 Theme Layout*. Activate **BookStore | Building Knowledge** in the admin area (http://localhost/packt/admin_packt) to see the result so far:

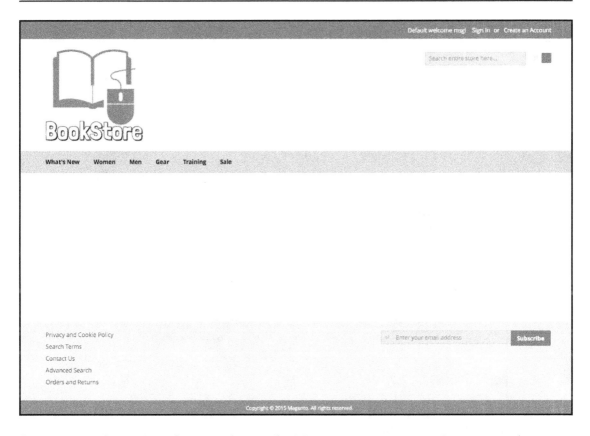

Sometimes, when you make an update to the Magento structure or activate a new theme, you need to deploy the changes. Here's how to deploy your changes:

1. Open a terminal or Command Prompt window.
2. Delete the `packt/pub/static/frontend/<Vendor>/<theme>/<locale>` directory.
3. Delete the `var/cache` directory (if present).
4. Delete the `var/view_preprocessed` directory.
5. Run the `php bin/magento setup:static-content:deploy` command.

In some cases, it is necessary to provide write permissions to the directories again.

Adding content with Magento CMS

Once the new theme has been activated, it's time to handle the content of your Magento 2 installation by creating some options and configuring products and categories.

To create new categories, you will need to access the admin area (`http://localhost/packt/admin_packt`) and follow these instructions:

1. Navigate to the **Products** | **Categories** menu.
2. Delete all the subcategories of the **Default Category** by clicking on them and pressing the **Delete Category** button.
3. Create the following three new subcategories under the **Default Category**: **Business**, **Science**, and **Technology**. Be sure to set the **Include in Navigation Menu** option to **YES** for each category.

In **Add Category**, you have options to fill the **Description**, **Page Title**, and **Meta Information** for SEO purposes:

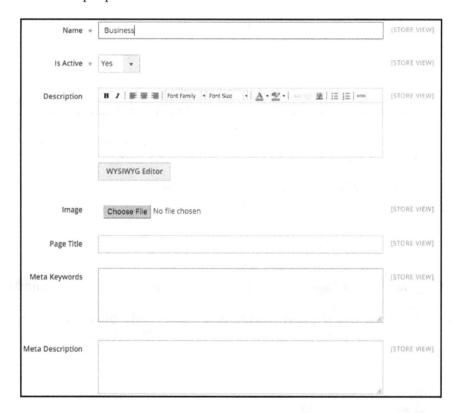

To create new products in your Magento 2 installation, follow these steps:

1. Navigate to **Products | Catalog**.
2. Click on the **Add Product** button.
3. On the **New Product** page, enter all the required **Product Information**.
4. Set **Price**, **Quantity**, and **Categories**.
5. Choose an image to upload.
6. Choose **In Stock** for the **Stock Availability** field.
7. Choose **Main Website** on the **Websites** tab.
8. Enable the product (**PRODUCT ONLINE**).
9. Save the new product.
10. You can add nine products for test purposes.

Take a look at the following screenshot:

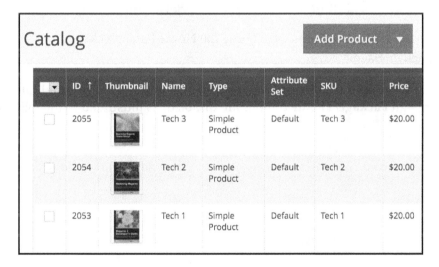

Displaying featured categories on the home page

Magento 2 has a widget management system that allows great flexibility of content disposal. For the BookStore theme, the widget will help create a specific list of new products on the home page.

Here's how to create a new widget in the admin area:

1. Navigate to **Content | Widgets**.
2. Click on the **Add Widget** button.
3. Set the **Type** as **CMS Static Block** and **Design Theme** as **BookStore | Building Knowledge** to continue the widget creation.
4. On **Storefront Properties** tab, type **Home Page** as the **Widget Title**. Choose the **All Store Views** option.
5. Add a **Layout Update** with these options:

   1. Display on: Specified Page.

   2. Page: CMS Home Page.

   3. Container: Main Content Area.

   4. Template: CMS Static Block Default Template.

6. On the **Widget Options** tab, choose the **Home Page** block.
7. Click on **Save**.

When you fill in the options to create your new widget to show the featured categories, the **Type** and **Design Package/Theme** options are disabled, as illustrated in the following screenshot:

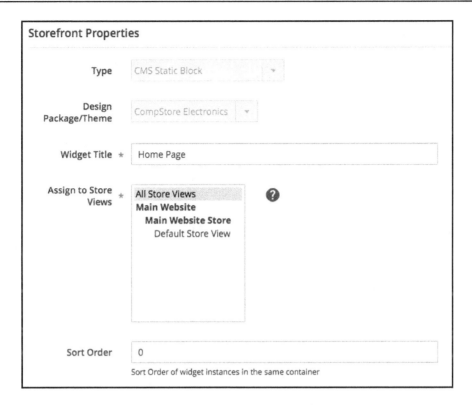

In the **Widgets** list, you can apply a filter to see the widget created only for a specific **Design Theme**, as illustrated in the following screenshot:

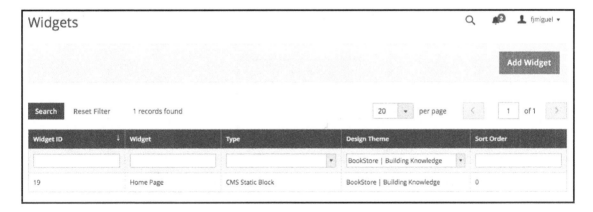

As seen in the *Magento 2 system layout* section in Chapter 3, *Magento 2 Theme Layout*, the system provides flexibility in inserting content once the theme has the element positions defined. It has been defined in such a way that the created block will be part of the **Main Content Area** of BookStore theme. Recall that the BookStore theme inherits the Luma theme attributes and behaviors.

If you browse the home page of your project, you will see that the block is already active but with the Luma theme's content information. To change this behavior, you need to edit the contents of the newly created block:

1. Navigate to **Content | Blocks**.
2. Click to edit the **Home Page** block.
3. In the **Content** field, enter the following HTML:

```
<div class="blocks-promo">
<a class="block-promo home-main" href="{{store
url=""}}technology.html">
<img src="{{media url="wysiwyg/home-main.jpg"}}" alt="" />
<span class="content bg-white">
<span class="info">New Books available!</span>
<strong class="title">New Brands</strong>
<span class="action more button">Shop New Books!</span> </span>
</a>
</div>
<div class="content-heading">
<h2 class="title">New Products</h2>
<p class="info">Here is what`s trending on BookStore now</p>
```

4. Position the cursor below the last line of HTML code, and click on the **Insert Widget** icon:

5. Choose **Catalog Products List** under **Widget Type**.

6. Choose in **Conditions** the featured categories created earlier:

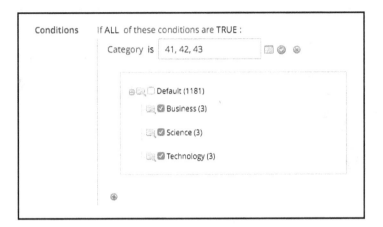

7. Click on the **Insert Widget** button.
8. If you prefer, you can create a new `home-main.jpg` image of size 1280 x 460 px and change the block:

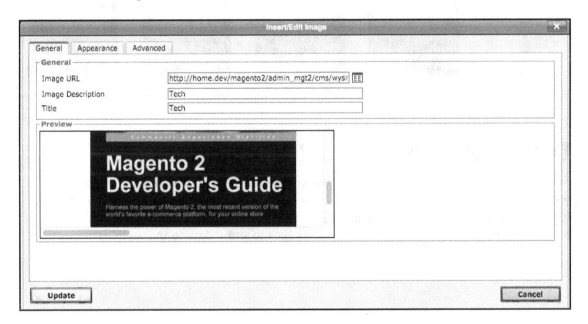

9. Click on the **Save Block** button.

Go to the home page to see the new update running:

Developing Magento 2 templates

Magento works with `.phtml` template files to generate the view layer for the users. Files with the `.phtml` extension contain both embedded HTML5 as well as PHP programming logic to render all page content using Magento processing. The modules and themes in Magento have their specific groups of `.phtml` files to show data to the users.

In an order to strengthen these concepts, it's time to implement some template development on the BookStore theme project by following these instructions:

1. Create the `Magento_Catalog` directory under the `app/design/frontend/Packt/bookstore` directory.

2. Copy the `vendor/magento/module_catalog/view/frontend/templates` directory to `app/design/frontend/Packt/bookstore/Magento_Catalog`.

3. Open the `app/design/frontend/Packt/bookstore/Magento_Catalog/templates/product/view/addto.phtml` file in your favorite code editor.

4. Go to line 17 and enter the following code: `<div><h2>Buy in BookStore!!!</h2></div>`

```
11  <?php
12  $_product = $block->getProduct();
13  $_wishlistSubmitParams =
    $this->helper('Magento\Wishlist\Helper\Data')->getAddParams($_product);
14  $compareHelper = $this->helper('Magento\Catalog\Helper\Product\Compare');
15  ?>
16
17  <div><h2>Buy in BookStore!!!</h2></div>
18  <div class="product-addto-links" data-role="add-to-links">
19      <?php if ($this->helper('Magento\Wishlist\Helper\Data')->isAllow()) : ?>
20          <a href="#"
21              class="action towishlist"
22              data-post='<?php /* @escapeNotVerified */ echo $_wishlistSubmitParams; ?>'
23              data-action="add-to-wishlist"><span><?php /* @escapeNotVerified */ echo __('Add to
                Wish List') ?></span></a>
24      <?php endif; ?>
```

5. Save the file.
6. Delete the `var/view_preprocessed/` and `pub/static/frontend/Packt/bookstore/` directories.
7. Deploy the `static-content` files by running `php magento setup:static-content:deploy`.
8. If necessary, give write permissions to the `pub` directory

Access any BookStore product to view the result of applying the new template and the result of applying the new CSS rules to the category page:

Here's what it does to the product page:

Each Magento 2 module manages your own frontend standardization of files: .less, media and JavaScript. If you navigate to the vendor/magento/theme-frontend-luma directory, you can check all the native modules available in Magento for a better understanding.

If you check the Magento_Theme directory, which has the role of managing the entire theme behavior in question, you will see that it has a directory called web/css/source. This directory contains the _module.less file, where you will find CSS code for the module to be rendered in the system. If you want to make changes, just create the module folder on your specific project directory, following the same naming conventions for directories and files and making necessary adjustments.

Explore the options that the high modularity of Magento 2 provides you! The more you apply what is learned at different levels of training and customization, the more solid your concepts will be! Perform a test by changing some other module and observing the result.

Summary

In this chapter, you created your first Magento 2 theme using the most powerful features that the LESS technology infrastructure allows. This does not necessarily mean that this is the end point; this is the starting point for creating Magento 2 themes with your own signature.

The application of techniques such as the Magento UI, developing Magento templates, and reusing code shows that the Magento 2 development professional who has a solid base and really understands the gear, that is, the communication of the main layers that render the Magento frontend, remains at a high level of professionalism.

In the next chapter, you will see how to debug your developed styles. See you!

6
Magento 2 Styles Debugging

"Writing software is a very intense, very personal thing. You have to have time to work your way through it, to understand it. Then debug it."
– Vinton Gray Cerf, American Internet pioneer, recognized as one of "the fathers of the Internet."

Surely you have noticed, dear reader, that although the techniques learned so far have been simple to understand, the process seems complicated once a simple change demands repetitive tasks, such as clearing directory static files, clearing the cache, or running the new deployment. It does not seem like much at first, but in a professional environment, where productivity is one of the keys to success, you need to create a workflow that attends to all expectations. This chapter will establish a new workflow that, from now on, will be used to develop Magento 2 theme projects by effectively debugging the changes that are proposed. The following topics are covered in this chapter:

- Increasing productivity by creating flow test styles
- Debugging styles in Magento
- Client-side debugging mode
- Server-side debugging mode
- Using the Grunt task runner for debugging
- Applying changes to BookStore with Grunt

Increasing productivity by creating flow test styles

As with any software development segment related to **agile development**, which is used a lot today to ensure quality and value in short cyclic periods, it's necessary to seek ways to implement improvements in every cycle.

Speaking specifically about **scrum** (`https://www.scrumalliance.org`), there is a component called **sprint retrospective**, in which we analyze what worked as well as what did not happen in the project-development flow. After this discussion, we propose improvements for the next delivery cycle. Besides the continuous delivery of quality features, the methodology should encourage the incremental improvement of its processes in order to increase productivity.

Following this idea and now that you have had an introduction to the construction techniques of a Magento 2 theme development, you can see that there are improvements that can be implemented in the process. Until now, the process for implementing theme changes from changes that have been made on the issues has been long and manual .

Is there a better way to manage these changes in the topic? The answer is yes, and you will implement an improvement in the process now!

Debugging styles in Magento

As described in `Chapter 4`, *Magento UI Library*, Magento 2 offers two ways to compile LESS technology:

- Server-side compilation
- Client-side compilation

Both techniques work in different ways when it comes to workflow development issues, especially when debugging code in an agile and interactive way. Let's explore the two methods of compiling styles and understand how they behave with theme-debugging solutions.

Client-side debugging mode

Client-side debugging on Magento 2 uses the `less.js` native library. This library uses the rules of in-browser LESS compilation, meant for development environments where the library JavaScript file is too big and its behavior of prioritizing the processing before rendering can generate a feeling of slowness for the user accessing the page. Basically, the `less.js` library is declared as follows:

```
<script src="less.js"></script>
```

 Refer to the documentation for how to use LESS on the client side: `http:/ /lesscss.org/usage/#using-less-in-the-browser`

When using this type of compilation, most of the changes that are applied to the theme will be readily applied when the page is reloaded, firing the reading process of the `less.js` library for every new rendering. To test this approach using the client-side LESS library-compilation mode, let's first activate the mode:

1. Access the administrative area (`http://localhost/packt/admin_packt`).
2. On the Magento **Admin** page, navigate to **Stores** | **Configuration** | **ADVANCED** | **Developer**.
3. In **Store View**, select **Default Config**.
4. Under **Front-end development workflow**, select **Client-side less compilation**.
5. Click on **Save Config**.

Take a look at the following screenshot:

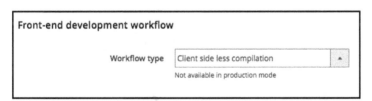

Now remove the static files we processed before, and generate a new deployment:

1. Delete the `<magento_root>/pub/static/frontend/<Vendor>/<theme>/<locale>`, `var/cache` and `var/view_preprocessed` directories.
2. Open a terminal or Command Prompt window.

3. Access the `<magento_root>/bin` directory.

4. Run `php magento setup:static-content:deploy`.

5. In some cases, it is necessary to provide write permissions to the directories again.

> To learn more about permission files, access the Magento 2 official documentation: `http://devdocs.magento.com/guides/v2.0/install-g` `de/prereq/file-system-perms.html`

Once client-side debugging has been enabled, test the following change to the Bookstore theme:

1. Open your favorite code editor.

2. Open the `app/design/frontend/Packt/bookstore/web/css/source/_theme.less` file and update lines one to nine with the following code:

```
@bookstore-background: #cccccc;
@primary__color: @color-white;
@page__background-color: @bookstore-background;
@sidebar__background-color: @color-black;
@border-color__base: @color-black;
@link__color: @color-white;
@link__hover__color: @color-black;
```

3. Reload the Magento frontend to see the result.

At this point, any changes you perform will be available instantly as soon as the page is reloaded. Perform tests with this new approach, and then return to the original code. Also note that the pages are slower to render content even if you are working on the localhost. This kind of approach is only meant for individual cases and, in some cases, you must remove the static content and generate a new deployment for the changes to have the desired effect.

When you change any content in the root source files that contain the `@magento_import` policy, for example, you should remove the `pub/static/frontend/<Vendor>/<Theme>/<Locale>` folder and generate a new deployment, as we saw in `Chapter 4`, *Magento UI Library*, and `Chapter 5`, *Creating a Responsive Magento 2 Theme*.

The `@magento_import` directive is a specific directive of LESS that assists the inclusion of multiple files available in different locations in order to integrate CSS and LESS files.

Official documentation about CSS preprocessing is available here: `http://devdocs.magento.com/guides/v2.0/frontend-dev-guide/css-topics/css-preprocess.html`

Server-side debugging mode

By default, Magento 2 uses LESS server-side compilation in order to optimize page rendering time for the user. For production environments, server-side compilation is preferred. This approach was used in previous chapters to update and change CSS files from both the HelloWorld and Bookstore themes, making it necessary to always create a new deployment for each adjustment.

Despite the fact that client-side compilation is effective for instantly updating CSS/LESS themes, it proves inefficient when it comes to performance and availability once all LESS processing is up to the browser and for each new request as it was possible to test previously.

To enable server-side compilation, follow these steps:

1. Access your Magento 2 administrative area.
2. On the Magento Admin page, navigate to **Stores | Configuration | ADVANCED | Developer**.
3. In **Store View**, select **Default Config**.
4. Under **Front-end development workflow**, select **Server-side less compilation**.
5. Click on **Save Config**.

Once your new theme is in a production environment and published, you will need to create an effective mechanism for the changes to be as transparent as possible to the server.

Create a workflow of processes from planning updates to be made to deploying them because it involves a lot of work, as you may have seen. A technique/tool that facilitates the style update process and even helps debug your code is a **task runner**. Task runners make up a workflow layer automating intermediate processes and repetitive tasks such as as compilation, minification, linting, and unit testing.

To work with Magento 2 theme development, we will use the JavaScript task runner **Grunt** (`http://gruntjs.com/`), which we will look at in detail next.

Using the Grunt task runner to debug

Grunt is a task runner written in JavaScript that helps us automate tasks and increase productivity. On the official website, you have access to several plugins (`http://gruntjs.com/plugins`), so you can adjust the use of Grunt according to your needs:

Magento 2 already supports some written tasks in Grunt, but you must install it before you start your application in automation tasks. The Grunt library plugins are managed by **npm**, which is the Node.js package manager. Therefore, you must install Node.js to run Grunt tasks.

In the following subsections, we will look at how to install Node.js for your OS.

Learn more about Node.js (`https://nodejs.org/en/`) and how it is being used to create web applications projects in large scale non-relational databases (NoSQL).

Installing Node.js on Linux

The following instructions focus on two specific Linux distributions: Debian and Ubuntu. In case you have a different distribution, go to `https://nodejs.org/en/download/package-manager/` for more information.

Node.js is available in binary files for installing via a package manager. To download and start the installation, follow these steps:

1. Open a Linux terminal.
2. Run `curl -sL https://deb.nodesource.com/setup_4.x | sudo -E bash -`.
3. Run `sudo apt-get install -y nodejs`.
4. Run `sudo apt-get install -y build-essential` to install Node.js.
5. Run `node --version` to test the installation of Node.js.

You can also test the Node.js command line. Just run `node` in your terminal:

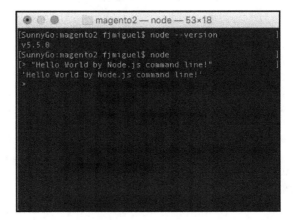

Installing Node.js on Windows

Here's how you install Node.js on Windows:

1. Go to the download page (`https://nodejs.org/en/download/`).
2. Choose the file corresponding to your architecture (32-bit or 64-bit).

3. Run the installation file and follow the steps to install Node.js.

Installing Node.js on OSX

You can directly download the installer for Mac available at `https://nodejs.org/en/#dow nload` or use the OSX package managers **Homebrew** (`http://brew.sh`) or **Macports** (`https ://www.macports.org`).

If you're using a package manager, keep this in mind:

- For Homebrew, run the `brew install node` command from the terminal
- For Macports, run `port install node`

Feel free to choose the option that best suits you!

 To test the Node.js installation, you can use `node --version` or `node` from your OSX terminal.

Installing Grunt

With the system prerequisites attended to, follow these steps to install Grunt:

1. Using a terminal or Command Prompt window, access the root directory of your Magento 2 installation.

2. Run `npm install -g grunt-cli`.

3. Run `npm install`.

4. Run `npm update`.

5. Open `<magento_root>/dev/tools/grunt/configs/themes.js` and enter the following code block inside the `module.exports={ }` statement:

```
bookstore: {
        area: 'frontend',
        name: 'Packt/bookstore',
        locale: 'en_US',
        files: [
                'css/styles-m',
                'css/styles-l'
        ],
        dsl: 'less'
    },
```

The main function of the `themes.js` file is establishing a connection between the scripts of the theme and the Grunt task runner, aiming to automate tasks when the theme has been finished. Also note that the file is already present in the default Magento themes collection for both the frontend and the administrative area. The final code file will be as follows:

```
module.exports = {
    blank: {
        area: 'frontend',
        name: 'Magento/blank',
        locale: 'en_US',
        files: [
            'css/styles-m',
            'css/styles-l',
            'css/email',
            'css/email-inline'
        ],
        dsl: 'less'
    },
    luma: {
        area: 'frontend',
        name: 'Magento/luma',
        locale: 'en_US',
```

```
        files: [
            'css/styles-m',
            'css/styles-l'
        ],
        dsl: 'less'
    },
    bookstore: {
        area: 'frontend',
        name: 'Packt/bookstore',
        locale: 'en_US',
        files: [
            'css/styles-m',
            'css/styles-l'
        ],
        dsl: 'less'
    },
    backend: {
        area: 'adminhtml',
        name: 'Magento/backend',
        locale: 'en_US',
        files: [
            'css/styles-old',
            'css/styles'
        ],
        dsl: 'less'
    }
};
```

The `module.exports` instruction, commonly used in Node.js, encapsulates the code unit that represents an object that can be taken to any JavaScript that is running on the same application framework. In this case, it is about a JSON statement that contains parameters that are loaded into the Grunt task runner.

> Read more about `module.exports` on the official Node.js documentation, available at `https://nodejs.org/api/modules.html` and to learn more about JSON data interchange access, visit `http://json.org/`.

Testing Grunt

The idea of testing Grunt using server-side compilation is to simulate an effective workflow for developing Magento themes using and configuring automation adjustments with minimum possible effort. In order to make development more dynamic, it is recommended you activate the cache system so that it participates in the new work process flow:

1. Open a terminal or Command Prompt window.
2. At the root folder of your Magento installation, run php bin/magento cache:enable.
3. You can check the status of the cache by running php bin/magento cache:status.

```
[SunnyGo:magento2 fjmiguel$ php bin/magento cache:status
Current status:
                        config: 1
                        layout: 1
                    block_html: 1
                   collections: 1
                    reflection: 1
                        db_ddl: 1
                           eav: 1
            config_integration: 1
        config_integration_api: 1
                     full_page: 1
                     translate: 1
             config_webservice: 1
```

Before using the commands to test the changes in the theme and workflow, do the following step by step:

1. Remove the pub/static/frontend/ and var/view_processed/source directories from your root directory.
2. Clear the cache with the php bin/magento cache:clean command.
3. Run the php bin/magento setup:static-content:deploy command.

Making a new deployment updates the LESS compilation system with information about the type of compilation (server-side compilation) and prevents errors that may occur when using Grunt for the first time.

All Grunt tasks will be done in a terminal or Command Prompt session, based on your operating system. It's possible to run the following tasks with Grunt to develop Magento 2 themes:

Command	Description
`grunt clean:<theme_name>`	Removes all static theme files in the `pub/static` folder and clears the cache and the files in the `view_processed` folder
`grunt deploy`	Makes a new deployment of all the themes in the `pub/static` folder
`grunt exec:<theme_name>`	Recreates all the symlinks (symbolic links/paths) for the `pub/static` pub directory of the theme
`grunt less:<theme_name>`	Compiles all CSS files from your theme using the referenced symlinks in the `pub/static` directory

Here's how to test the working of Grunt to simulate a change in the theme:

1. Open the `app/design/frontend/Packt/bookstore/web/css/source/_theme.less` file in your favorite code editor and update lines one to nine with the following code:

   ```
   @bookstore-background: #F0E68C;
   @primary__color: @color-black;
   @page__background-color: @bookstore-background;
   @sidebar__background-color: @color-gray40;
   @border-color__base: @color-gray76;
   @link__color: @color-white;
   @link__hover__color: @color-gray60;
   ```

2. Now follow these steps to test Grunt:

   1. Open a terminal or Command Prompt window.

   2. Run `grunt clean:bookstore`.

   3. Run `grunt exec:bookstore`.

   4. Run `grunt less:bookstore`.

3. Reload your website to see the changes:

```
[SunnyGo:magento2 fjmiguel$ grunt exec:bookstore
Running "exec:bookstore" (exec) task
Running "clean:bookstore" (clean) task
>> 0 paths cleaned.

Done, without errors.


Execution Time (2016-05-15 22:15:40 UTC)
loading tasks              247ms  ██████████████ 90%
loading grunt-contrib-clean  7ms  █ 3%
clean:bookstore             18ms  ██ 7%
Total 273ms

Processed Area: frontend, Locale: en_US, Theme: Packt/bookstore, File type: less.
-> css/styles-m.less
-> css/styles-l.less
Successfully processed.

Done, without errors.


Execution Time (2016-05-15 22:15:39 UTC)
loading tasks     240ms  █ 1%
exec:bookstore     22s   ████████████████████████████ 98%
Total 22.4s

[SunnyGo:magento2 fjmiguel$ grunt less:bookstore
Running "less:bookstore" (less) task
File pub/static/frontend/Packt/bookstore/en_US/css/styles-m.css created: 329 kB → 565.03 kB
File pub/static/frontend/Packt/bookstore/en_US/css/styles-l.css created: 97.41 kB → 166.58 kB

Done, without errors.
```

The `grunt clean:bookstore` command cleans the entire directory that contains the static and processed files of your theme. Once the cleaning is done, the `grunt exec:bookstore` command recreates all the symlinks of the theme, creating all the references that will be used on LESS files in the Magento system, specifically on themes. Finally, `grunt less:bookstore` reprocesses the LESS files to be rendered when the theme is loaded by the Magento system. Note that the process is much simpler than that used in previous chapters to edit and customize the theme style files. After the adjustments, three commands are enough to view the changes-simple, isn't it?

grunt watch

What if there were a yet simpler way? Once the workflow is configured and running, it can be used as an advantage of the project automation tool that currently gives support to the development of Magento 2 themes.

The `grunt watch` command automates all the three previous steps, requiring us to only load the page to view the result applied:

1. Open a terminal or Command Prompt session.
2. Run `grunt watch` and wait until you see `Waiting....`

3. Open the `_theme.less` file and change the block with the basic colors to the following:

```
@bookstore-background: #FF8C00;
@primary__color: @color-white;
@page__background-color: @bookstore-background;
@sidebar__background-color: @color-white;
@border-color__base: @color-black;
@link__color: @color-black;
@link__hover__color: @color-white;
```

Wait a few seconds until the files have been processed:

```
[SunnyGo:magento2 fjmiguel$ grunt watch
Running "watch" task
Waiting...
>> File "pub/static/frontend/Packt/bookstore/en_US/css/source/_theme.less" changed.
Running "less:bookstore" (less) task
File pub/static/frontend/Packt/bookstore/en_US/css/styles-m.css created: 328.93 kB → 565.14 kB
File pub/static/frontend/Packt/bookstore/en_US/css/styles-l.css created: 97.4 kB → 166.56 kB

Done, without errors.


Execution Time (2016-05-15 22:53:54 UTC)
loading tasks               259ms    ▉2%
loading grunt-contrib-less  552ms    ▉4%
less:bookstore              12.7s    ▉94%
Total 13.5s

Completed in 14.034s at Sun May 15 2016 19:54:07 GMT-0300 (BRT) - Waiting...
>> File "pub/static/frontend/Packt/bookstore/en_US/css/styles-m.css" changed.
>> File "pub/static/frontend/Packt/bookstore/en_US/css/styles-l.css" changed.
Completed in 0.000s at Sun May 15 2016 19:54:07 GMT-0300 (BRT) - Waiting...
>> File "pub/static/frontend/Packt/bookstore/en_US/css/source/_theme.less" changed.
Running "less:bookstore" (less) task
File pub/static/frontend/Packt/bookstore/en_US/css/styles-m.css created: 328.93 kB → 565.14 kB
File pub/static/frontend/Packt/bookstore/en_US/css/styles-l.css created: 97.4 kB → 166.56 kB

Done, without errors.


Execution Time (2016-05-15 22:54:25 UTC)
loading tasks   302ms    ▉2%
less:bookstore  14.4s    ▉97%
Total 14.8s
```

Reload your Magento website to see the changes applied:

Any changes from now on will be readily updated by the Grunt task runner, requiring you to only reload the page to view the applied customizations—much easier now! Run a test with this proposed flow. Discover improvements, and find your way. The important thing is to have this initial training so that you, dear reader, can develop quality themes for Magento 2 using a productive workflow.

Applying changes to Bookstore with Grunt

Using the new workflow and debug method, it is the time to make improvements to the Bookstore theme. Access the display page of any product you registered before, and see how the **Reviews** block looks now:

The colors are not well-suited to a white background, and there are some rendering errors in assigning stars to the product. To adjust this, make the following changes:

1. Run the `grunt watch` command. Open the `_theme.less` file from the Bookstore theme, and add the following CSS code to the end of the file:

```
body{color:@color-black;}
.breadcrumbs .items{color: #F56105;}
.review-control-vote:before{ content:@icon-star @icon-star @icon-
star   @icon-star @icon-star;}
```

2. Wait a few seconds until Grunt processes the files.
3. Reload the product page to view the result.

Take a look at the following screenshot:

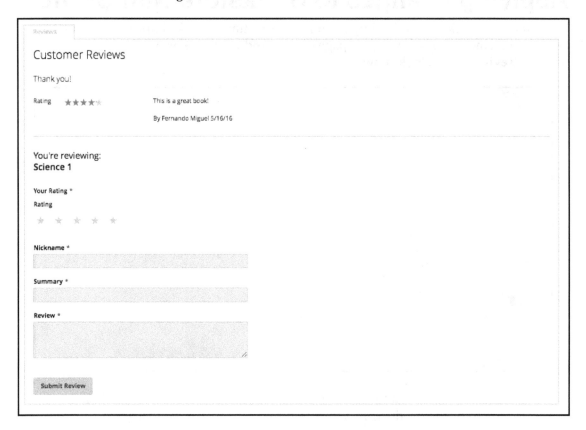

With minimum effort, you have made some important changes to the theme!

It's important to emphasize that the `.review-control-vote:before` class is using the Magento UI concept, previously seen in Chapter 4, *Magento UI Library*, to render the rating stars of the product through its icons library.

To check which icons are available for use in your projects through the Magento UI library, access the `<magento_root>/lib/web/css/source/lib/variables/_icons.less` file. As an exercise, try to change your product category page with the techniques learned so far. Use your creativity. Begin to shape the project so that it has the features you think are ideal!

Summary

In this chapter, we created mechanisms that enable you to achieve the highest possible productivity when developing Magento 2 themes, by automating repetitive tasks using the Grunt task runner.

I strongly suggest that you search for additional solutions on this topic so that you progressively optimize your way of working, generating higher value for and, consequently, quality in the final product that you want to deliver. In the next chapter, you will work with Magento UI components, which are a powerful approach for the enrichment of your Magento 2 themes. You will learn to work with the most common UI components. See you!

7
Magento UI Components

"There are two ways of constructing a software design: One way is to make it so simple that there are obviously no deficiencies and the other way is to make it so complicated that there are no obvious deficiencies." – C.A.R. Hoare, The 1980 ACM Turing Award Lecture.

Magento 2 uses resources to reuse elements that all developers work through good programming techniques. A great example is the Magento UI components. Every User Interface, specifically in the administrative area, has its basic elements present in almost all the different management pages.

You will see in this chapter how to use these elements in your projects and how the Magento 2 system provides the right tools so that these elements are used in different layouts.

The following topics are covered in this chapter:

- Magento UI components
- UI listing/grid component
- UI listing/grid secondary components
- Form component
- UI components control definition file
- Magento sample module form

The Magento UI components

The Magento UI components module was implemented to support the new approach of **User Experience (UX)**, which makes the new version of Magento 2 much more user-friendly than previous versions.

The main objective of this module is to promote the reuse of common components to any system that uses basic functions of the persistence database. Such functions can be listed as CREATE, READ, UPDATE, and DELETE, which popularized the term known as **CRUD**, symbolizing each of the actions for its initial letter.

This module is widely used in the administrative area of Magento 2, which obtained a natural evolution in UX, and it offers the possibility of working with item fragments to render the page and provides support to interactions between JavaScript components and servers.

Usually, the UI components module can be found on the `vendor` structure of the Magento 2 system. Open the `README.md` file, available at `<magento_root>/vendor/magento/module-ui`, to view the module objective:

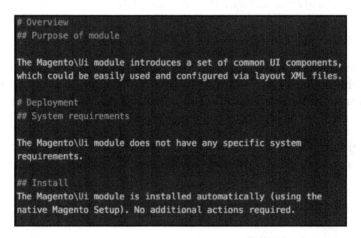

```
# Overview
## Purpose of module

The Magento\Ui module introduces a set of common UI components,
which could be easily used and configured via layout XML files.

# Deployment
## System requirements

The Magento\Ui module does not have any specific system
requirements.

## Install
The Magento\Ui module is installed automatically (using the
native Magento Setup). No additional actions required.
```

As you can see, this channel of communication between the layout and the reuse module components is done through XML layout files, as will be seen in the following chapter.

UI listing/grid component

The listing or data grid can be valued as the main function of any basic CRUD and it is necessary to have access to the contents present list in a given scope of access. See the example of the products **Catalog** list in the admin area:

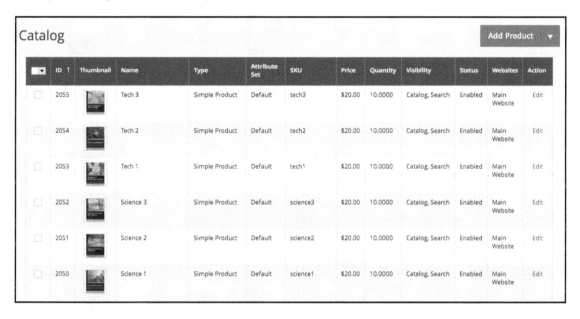

It's possible to see that this standard structure is used at different points of the administrative area of the Magento 2 system, but with a different scope of information according to the area being accessed.

It was necessary to standardize and normalize access to these components to generate a natural expansion resources and rendering elements. Just imagine if, for each theme's administration page, it was necessary to edit new HTML and CSS? It would be totally unproductive.

The listing component is responsible for promoting the filtering schemes of pagination, sorting, and upload inside lists, among other common actions of a system that uses CRUD.

Even though the native module is available in the directory `<magento_root>/vendor/magento/module-ui`, the UI components extend to other modules through the reuse of the code and statement in configuration files (xml), according to which the developer plans new implementations.

Looking at the products catalog, as previously seen, it checks that there is a component called **Mass Action**, shown in the following screenshot:

Mass Action can be used for more than one item from the catalog, automating some processes such as removing and changing items. This component is part of the UI components used specifically in the grid layer.

Open the file <magento_root>/vendor/magento/module-catalog/view/adminhtml/ui_component/product_listing.xml to observe Mass Action from line 84:

```
<massaction name="listing_massaction">
  <argument name="data" xsi:type="array">
    <item name="config" xsi:type="array">
      <item name="selectProvider" xsi:type="string">
        product_listing.product_listing.product_columns.ids
      </item>
      <item name="component" xsi:type="string">
        Magento_Ui/js/grid/tree-massactions
      </item>
      <item name="indexField" xsi:type="string">
        entity_id
      </item>
    </item>
  </argument>
  <action name="delete">
    <argument name="data" xsi:type="array">
      <item name="config" xsi:type="array">
        <item name="confirm" xsi:type="array">
          <item name="title" xsi:type="string" translate="true">
            Delete items
          </item>
          <item name="message" xsi:type="string" translate="true">
            Delete selected items?
          </item>
        </item>
        <item name="type" xsi:type="string">
          delete
        </item>
```

```
    <item name="label" xsi:type="string" translate="true">
      Delete
    </item>
    <item name="url" xsi:type="url" path="catalog/product/massDelete"/>
  </item>
  </argument>
</action>
...
</massaction>
```

In the preceding code section, the component Mass Action is being declared in the Magento administration area of the products catalog page. Note that the layout file is available in the `ui_component` directory, which in practice means that the Magento system processes the layout files of the modules and always searches for the same nomenclature of directories to check if there are, or are not, any statements of UI components.

Note that the layout file has a standard set to statements tags, parameters, and instructions to be used by the Magento system:

- `<massaction>`: Tag to start the use of Mass Action
- `<argument>`: Arguments used in the component as a declaration and indexing
- `<action>`: Represents an item from the tree of actions to be implemented as part of the UI component
- `<item>`: Parameterization of types and values according to the **XML Schema Instance (XSI)**

In the same file, the first lines of the following statement are declared:

```
<listing xmlns:xsi="http://www.w3.org/2001/XMLSchema-instance"
xsi:noNamespaceSchemaLocation="urn:magento:module:Magento_Ui:etc/ui_configu
ration.xsd">
```

For a better understanding of the standardization used in layout files, Magento 2 works with a **Uniform Resource Names (URN)** schema validation to reference XML declarations; and uses the **XML Schema Definition (XSD)** language for standardization and structuring of the UI component settings.

> To learn more, access the official documentation of W3C XML Schema at:
> `https://www.w3.org/TR/xmlschema11-1/`

As an exercise, navigate through the administrative modules and view how the statements of UI components are placed in the `ui-component` directory.

The name parameter, defined in the tag `<massaction name=" listing_massaction">`, is used to render the UI component in the View layer (frontend) of the administrative area using a single template defined in the UI module. Open the file `<magento_root>/vendor/magento/module-ui/view/base/web/templates/grid/toolbar.html` to view where it will be rendered in the Mass Action component from line 17:

```
...
<div class="admin__data-grid-header-row row row-gutter">
  <!-- ko if: hasChild('listing_massaction') -->
  <div class="col-xs-2" data-bind="scope:
requestChild('listing_massaction')">
    <!-- ko template: getTemplate() --><!-- /ko -->
  </div>
  <!-- /ko -->
  <div data-bind="css: {
    'col-xs-10': hasChild('listing_massaction'),
    'col-xs-12': !hasChild('listing_massaction')
  }">
    <div class="row">
      <div class="col-xs-3" data-bind="scope:
requestChild('listing_paging')">
        <!-- ko template: totalTmpl --><!-- /ko -->
      </div>
      <div class="col-xs-9" data-bind="scope:
requestChild('listing_paging')">
        <!-- ko template: getTemplate() --><!-- /ko -->
      </div>
    </div>
  </div>
</div>
...
```

Note the `requestChild` statement (`'listing_massaction'`), which indicates which tag will render the Mass Action component. In this way, any module that you want to use UI components in will be rendered in UI module templates reusing the code already implemented.

Through your research, you can find that when the Magento 2 native modules directories are quoted, they have the following notation `Magento/Sales/view/adminhtml/ui_component/`. In this book, you will notice that the complete path is used to point to the vendor directory. This is in order to be very clear of the path to which the example is available and to avoid errors. For more information, access the official documentation of Magento 2 at: `http://devdocs.magento.com/guides/v2.0/extension-dev-guide/build/module-file-structure.html`

UI listing/grid secondary components

The Mass Action component, as previously seen, extends the basic functionalities of **listing** components of UI components. It can then be called as a secondary component of UI components.

Other secondary components that make up the UI Components are:

- Filter
- Pagination
- TreeMass Action
- Column
- UI-select
- Multiselect
- Inline Edit
- Bookmark
- Resize
- Sticky header
- Export Button
- File Uploader

Each one has a specific function to create new elements using the reuse of predefined components. See the following sections for the specific functioning of each one of them.

Filter

The **filter** component aims to create filters to the listing that is displayed. In the previous example referring to the products catalog, it's possible to view the filter in action when it clicks the **Filters** tab:

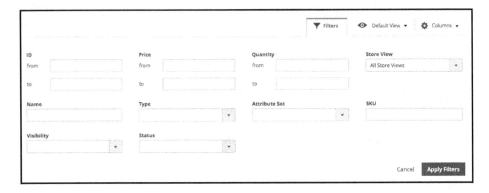

Pagination

A standard component for any CRUD defines the simple rules of list pagination being displayed. By default, this component works with the amount of items being displayed per page and the navigation page number:

TreeMass action

Extends Mass Action functionalities creating a nested menu. Here is an example of application in the Magento clients system management section:

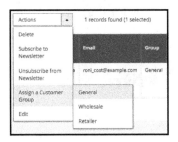

Column

The **Column** component provides the display functionality for the columns that the user wants to appear in the listing. This is very useful when users want to obtain specific and punctual crossing data, as seen in the following example:

UI-select

The UI-select component provides the option of using a column selection filter with up to three levels without the need to use a checkbox. It is only necessary to select the option so that it is already active in the field, as seen in the following example:

Multiselect

The **Multiselect** component extends the Column components functionalities, enabling a multiple selection option of the checkbox's specific elements list. To understand the operation of this component, simply view the operation of the Column component to understand its scope.

Inline edit

Enables an **inline** editing option of a list element. This is useful when you want to change an element in an agile manner, without the need to enter into a particular detailing page. See the following component application example in user management:

Bookmark

The **bookmark** component allows for active and changed data from the grid to be stored including filters, columns, ordination, and paging. It uses the database to record the latest states. This kind of functionality makes it easier for the user because there is no additional work to re-apply the options selected.

To test its operation, simply apply any filter rule or even paging and reload the page with the CRUD that you are accessing. When the page is available again you will notice that the last components that you used will still be shown with the latest options selected.

Resize

With this component it is possible, via layout file parameterization, to set the size of the column according to what you plan for the UI solution for your project and even for your module.

To better understand the operation as a UI component, open the file
`<magento_root>/vendor/magento/module-cms/view/adminhtml/ui_component/cms_page_listing.xml` and see how the **Resize** is applied from line 388:

```
<actionsColumn name="actions"
class="Magento\Cms\Ui\Component\Listing\Column\PageActions">
<argument name="data" xsi:type="array">
<item name="config" xsi:type="array">
<item name="resizeEnabled" xsi:type="boolean">false</item>
        <item name="resizeDefaultWidth" xsi:type="string">
107
</item>
        <item name="indexField" xsi:type="string">
page_id
</item>
    </item>
  </argument>
</actionsColumn>
```

Setting the behavior of the actions column in the `actionsColumn` tag, it is possible to parameterize configuration items related to the column resize. The `resizeEnabled` and the `resizeDefaultWidth`, for example, define respectively that the column will not be resizable and will have the default width of `107` pixels.

Sticky header

The **Sticky Header** component allows the header of your listing to be fixed at the top of your page while vertical navigation occurs on the available items in the list. This is very useful when applied to a list with a large number of items.

In the same `cms_page_listing.xml` file, previously used as an example of the resize component, see how this component is applied:

```
<argument name="data" xsi:type="array">
<item name="config" xsi:type="array">
    <item name="template" xsi:type="string">ui/grid/toolbar</item>
    <item name="stickyTmpl" xsi:type="string">
ui/grid/sticky/toolbar
 </item>
  </item>
</argument>
```

Through the template and `stickyTmpl` parameters, it is possible to enter the component in your UI proposal. To test the operation of this component, navigate to the administrative area **Content** | **Pages**:

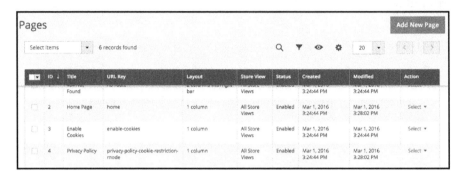

Export button

The **Export** button provides the export data functionality from your data grid in CSV and XML mainly. It is very used to data exportation requests made , for example.

See how simple it is to implement this functionality in your grid data:

```
<exportButton name="export_button">
<argument name="data" xsi:type="array">
        <item name="config" xsi:type="array">
         <item name="selectProvider" xsi:type="string">
sales_order_grid.sales_order_grid.sales_order_columns.ids
</item>
        </item>
</argument>
</exportButton>
```

This code segment was taken from the file `<magento_root>/vendor/magento/module-sales/view/adminhtml/ui_component/sales_order_grid.xml` and aims to promote an export component to the requests section received in the administrative area:

File uploader

The **File uploader** component provides the file upload option in the UI Components and acts as an adapter of the JQuery File Upload plugin. This component is a complement of the Form component, which will be presented in the following chapter. Its statement as a UI component is made as follows:

```
<argument name="data" xsi:type="array">
<item name="config" xsi:type="array">
    <item name="label" xsi:type="string">Upload My File</item>
        <item name="visible" xsi:type="boolean">true</item>
        <item name="formElement" xsi:type="string">fileUploader</item>
        <item name="uploaderConfig" xsi:type="array">
          <item name="url" xsi:type="url" path="path/to/controller"/>
        </item>
    </item>
...
</argument>
```

The `formElement` and `uploaderConfig` parameters import the component and define which controller will be responsible for processing the file.

For more information about secondary components, please refer to the Magento official documentation available at: `http://devdocs.magento.com/guides/v2.0/ui-components/ui-secondary.html`

Form component

Until now we have presented components that take care of all the data grid exhibition with regard to filtering, paging, navigation, and even functionality to temporary recording parameters (Bookmark). Beside all these elements that provide indispensable functionalities to a data grid, it is necessary to have a specific component that takes care of CRUD operations on specific elements of the grid. This is the **Form component** scope of action.

In the previous section of this chapter, it was possible to observe that the File uploader component integrates part of the Form component scope so that it is a common item to HTML forms.

The following components extend the functionalities of the Form component:

- DataSource
- FieldSet
- Field
- Layout
- Container

To better understand this dynamic, make an analysis of the configuration file definition responsible for forms management of the customer module in Magento 2. Open the file `<magento_root>/vendor/magento/module-customer/view/base/ui_component/customer_form.xml` and observe the following operating logic:

```
customer_form.xml        x
49      <fieldset name="customer">
50          <argument name="data" xsi:type="array">
51              <item name="config" xsi:type="array">
52                  <item name="label" xsi:type="string" translate="true">Account Information</item>
53              </item>
54          </argument>
55          <field name="entity_id">
56              <argument name="data" xsi:type="array">
57                  <item name="config" xsi:type="array">
58                      <item name="visible" xsi:type="boolean">false</item>
59                      <item name="dataType" xsi:type="string">text</item>
60                      <item name="formElement" xsi:type="string">input</item>
61                      <item name="source" xsi:type="string">customer</item>
62                  </item>
63              </argument>
64          </field>
65          <field name="created_in">
66              <argument name="data" xsi:type="array">
67                  <item name="config" xsi:type="array">
68                      <item name="visible" xsi:type="boolean">false</item>
69                      <item name="formElement" xsi:type="string">input</item>
70                      <item name="source" xsi:type="string">customer</item>
71                  </item>
72              </argument>
73          </field>
```

- The `<form>` tag is declared using the URN patterns of Magento UI
- In the tag `<argument>` it is possible to visualize the initial layout settings and also the buttons that will be part of the forms
- Then `<dataSource>` is defined, which aims to parameterize the recording layer and validation of persisted data in the form
- In the tags `<fieldset>` and `<field>` a grouping of form fields and definitions of inputs, respectively, occurs
- Through the `<container>` it is possible to group the fieldsets and the form fields in the same scope inside the system

At first it seems a little complicated, but it is simpler to deepen these concepts when it is possible to understand both the logic application and what benefits it can bring to developers.

It's necessary to understand these initial concepts to take advantage of the good practice that can be applied in developing new layouts to modules and even to your theme.

For more information, access the Magento 2 official documentation available at: `http://devdocs.magento.com/guides/v2.0/ui-component s/ui-form.html`

UI components control definition file

All of these items listed as UI components are managed by the UI module. The UI Module centralizes the statements in the file `<magento_root>/vendor/magento/module-ui/view/base/ui_component/etc/definiton.xml`, which are available with all UI components, represented by the following code segment:

```xml
definition.xml                    x
<?xml version="1.0" encoding="UTF-8"?>
<!--
/**
 * Copyright © 2016 Magento. All rights reserved.
 * See COPYING.txt for license details.
 */
-->
<components xmlns:xsi="http://www.w3.org/2001/XMLSchema-instance"
    xsi:noNamespaceSchemaLocation="urn:magento:module:Magento_Ui:etc/ui_definition.xsd">
    <dataSource class="Magento\Ui\Component\DataSource"/>
    <listing sorting="true" class="Magento\Ui\Component\Listing">
        <argument name="data" xsi:type="array">
            <item name="template" xsi:type="string">templates/listing/default</item>
            <item name="save_parameters_in_session" xsi:type="string">1</item>
            <item name="client_root" xsi:type="string">mui/index/render</item>
            <item name="config" xsi:type="array">
                <item name="component" xsi:type="string">uiComponent</item>
            </item>
        </argument>
    </listing>
```

The UI module searches in all modules to see if there is a new statement or a call for the UI components on the `ui_component` directory, as previously seen. This same rule applies to the `definition.xml` configuration file, in case you want to have a specific configuration in your module.

This case is applicable only if you want to customize the UI components functionalities in a global way. For adjustments and punctual statements it is recommended to follow the notation demonstrated in this chapter through the following application examples:

```
<module_root>/<vendor>/<module>/view/<area>/ui_component/<component_instance_name>.xml
```

For more information, access the Magento 2 official documentation about UI components, available at: `http://devdocs.magento.com/guides/v2.0/ui-components/ui-component.html`

Magento sample module form

This book's scope is not Magento 2 backend development, but to complement the examples given in relation to the UI components in a succinct way, it is advisable to implement a complete solution only with the techniques learned in this chapter.

To fulfill this context, the Magento team maintains a GitHub repository of its community edition solutions. This repository is available at `https://github.com/magento` and it is possible to find several samples of Magento modules and documentations:

A sample UI component application, called **Sample Module Form** is also available (`https://github.com/magento/magento2-samples/tree/master/sample-module-form-uicomponent`). This is a great example that includes integration of backend and frontend and gives to you a clear idea of how it works with the UI components module. Please download the Sample Module Form and follow the step-by-step instructions for the module installation:

1. Download or clone the repository.
2. Create the `directory /app/code/Magento/SampleForm`.
3. Copy the contents of the directory `sample-module-form-uicomponent` to the `/app/code/Magento/SampleForm`.

4. Run the command `php bin/magento setup:upgrade` on the terminal or from the Command Prompt.

5. Run the command `php bin/magento module:enable Magento_SampleForm` on the terminal or from the Command Prompt.

After these steps, access the administrative area of your Magento installation, then login and type `http://localhost/packt/admin_packt/sampleform` into the address bar of your navigator to see the following result:

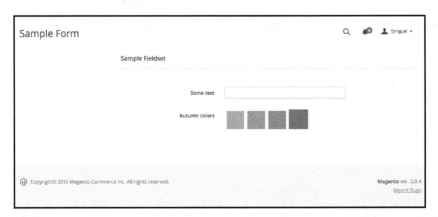

Navigate to the directory to which you copied the Sample Form module and open the file `view/adminhtml/ui_component/sampleform_form.xml` to see the implementation of the UI component. Observe the code segment in action according to the techniques discussed in this chapter:

```
...
<field name="color">
<argument name="data" xsi:type="array">
        <item name="config" xsi:type="array">
            <item name="component" xsi:type="string">
Magento_SampleForm/js/form/element/color-select
</item>
<item name="template" xsi:type="string">
ui/form/field
</item>
<item name="elementTmpl" xsi:type="string">
Magento_SampleForm/form/element/color-select
</item>
            <item name="label" xsi:type="string">Autumn colors</item>
<item name="visible" xsi:type="boolean">true</item>
<item name="dataType" xsi:type="string">text</item>
<item name="formElement" xsi:type="string">input</item>
```

```
<item name="source" xsi:type="string">sampleform</item>
</item>
</argument>
</field>
...
```

I suggest that you navigate throughout the module structure to understand its dynamics beyond the UI components.

Access the Magento PHP Developers for more information about the modules development, available at `http://devdocs.magento.com/guide s/v2.0/extension-dev-guide/bk-extension-dev-guide.html`.

Summary

Despite this book's scope not being about backend development, it is very important that the Magento frontend developer has a minimum understanding of how the Magento system complements the rendering of pages and how the interaction between backend and frontend works, and to have the minimum knowledge to aggregate more value to your project.

In this chapter, you saw how the UI Components module can be used in several layout proposals, and how it's possible to reuse the basic elements of data grid, forms, and actions involving a basic CRUD. You now also have knowledge of how the configuration files can help in the declaration of these elements in the layout proposal.

In the next chapter, the concepts of Magento 2 layout development for themes will be developed further.

8
Magento Layout Development

"Anyone who slaps a 'this page is best viewed with Browser X' label on a web page appears to be yearning for the bad old days, before the Web, when you had very little chance of reading a document written on another computer, another word processor, or another network." -Tim Berners-Lee.

You have obtained the basics of use and code fragments, but from now on you will make practical applications by creating blocks, containers, and manipulation schemes layout configuration files to the development of the Magento themes.

The following topics will be covered in the chapter:

- Magento page layout
- Layout instructions and types
- Layout customizations
- Customizing templates

The Magento page layout

As seen in `Chapter 2`, *Exploring Magento Themes*, Magento 2 was written using the **MVC** architecture. The adoption of this pattern is shown to be very effective because of the complexity of the Magento system and it also provides greater understanding of the development necessary to extend the native functionalities represented by modules, customizations, and themes.

In the **View** layer, specifically, there is the predominant application layout schemes. The layout is nothing more than a page structure that can be represented by a hierarchy of elements that can be represented both as blocks and as containers.

All layout blocks or pages that enable the rendering of the HTML page, are named as layout handles. The layout handles are used to define the nomenclature of the files and are divided into three types:

- **Page type layout handles**: Corresponds to the controller name and actions in its totality. For example, `customer_view`.
- **Page layout handles**: These are used as a specific page's identifiers via parameters. For example, `catalog_product_view_type_simple_id_31`.
- **Arbitrary handles**: These do not correspond to any specific item of the controller, but are included as support for other handles.

In `Chapter 7`, *Magento UI Components*, the definition of layout structures was used through XML settings files whose content is declared with parameters and manipulating elements. But what is the process to create specific layouts in the development of themes for Magento?

More layout concepts will be studied and you will make more punctual tests in the Bookstore theme by applying the techniques explained.

The page layout is a powerful technique because it allows for the creation of specific elements in the design of your theme. In the sequence you will have more contact with this technique.

Layout instructions and types

There are two different ways to customize a layout on your Magento project. The first is to change the layout configuration files (XML) as was done in `Chapter 7`, *Magento UI Components*. The second is to change the template files (phtml) as well, as tested in Chapter 5, *Creating a Responsive Magento 2 Theme*.

The layout configuration files are specially used to change the position of a wireframe elements page such as header, content, and footer to define which elements will be displayed at each point of the layout. Therefore, it is possible to control behaviors, adding and/or removing elements in a compartmentalized manner.

The layout configuration files have the following instructions in tags format and attributes, for manipulation of elements:

- `<block>`: Refers to the specific block of content that can be in HTML format and uses templates (phtml) to render its contents

- `<container>`: Groups elements that can be blocks and even other containers
- `before` and `after` attributes: Attributes are used to define the display order of blocks and containers
- `<referenceBlock>` and `<referenceContainer>`: Allows you to create references to blocks that you have already created earlier, even if the blocks belongs to other layout configuration files
- `<move>`: Allows you to move a block or container inside another block or container
- `<remove>`: Removes static elements, such as CSS and JS, particularly header blocks or containers
- `<update>`: Includes a new template in the block or container
- `<argument>`: Makes the transfer of arguments to the template directly

Here is an application example of the configuration file, `catalog_product_index.xml`:

```
<?xml version="1.0"?>
<page xmlns:xsi="http://www.w3.org/2001/XMLSchema-instance"
xsi:noNamespaceSchemaLocation="urn:magento:framework:View/Layout/etc/page_c
onfiguration.xsd">
    <update handle="styles"/>
    <body>
        <referenceBlock name="menu">
            <action method="setActive">
                <argument name="itemId" xsi:type="string">
Magento_Catalog::catalog_products
</argument>
            </action>
        </referenceBlock>
        <referenceBlock name="page.title">
            <action method="setTitleClass">
             <argument name="class" xsi:type="string">
complex
</argument>
            </action>
        </referenceBlock>
        <referenceContainer name="content">
            <uiComponent name="product_listing"/>
            <block class="Magento\Catalog\Block\Adminhtml\Product"
name="products_list"/>
        </referenceContainer>
    </body>
</page>
```

In the previous example, the layout configuration page file treats all the elements of the exhibition logic in the `Catalog` module in the administrative page of Magento 2. Basically, this configuration file creates references to the `blocks` menu and `page.title`, transferring arguments to be used in each of the blocks. It also references the content container and defines the UI component `product_listing` in the product block.

Throughout this chapter, these concepts will be applied for further understanding. It is interesting to keep a catalog for consultation and to be always updated on the news available within the official documentation.

 For more information, please access the official Magento documentation: h ttp://devdocs.magento.com/guides/v2.0/frontend-dev-guide/layou ts/xml-instructions.html

For each page/template are available three types of layout files:

- **Page layout**: The main objective is to set the page skeleton. For example, it defines if the rendered layout has one, two, or three columns for displaying the content.
- **Page configuration**: Defines the structure of the page and which files will be added to render the pages.
- **Generic Layout**: Responsible for the availability and visualization of the elements in the body page in a detailed manner.

Extend and override a layout

The Magento system provides two ways to customize the page layout files in your project: extend or override the file.

In the example of `Chapter 3`, *Magento 2 Theme Layout*, the `default.xml` layout file was used to change the logo file of the main theme:

```
<page xmlns:xsi="http://www.w3.org/2001/XMLSchema-instance"
xsi:noNamespaceSchemaLocation="urn:magento:framework:View/Layout/etc/page_c
onfiguration.xsd">
    <body>
        <referenceBlock name="logo">
            <arguments>
                <argument name="logo_file" xsi:type="string">
Magento_Theme/images/logo.png
  </argument>
                <argument name="logo_img_width" xsi:type="number">
```

```
238
 </argument>
 <argument name="logo_img_height" xsi:type="number">
219
 </argument>
            </arguments>
        </referenceBlock>
    </body>
</page>
```

This was only possible due to the extend layout technique to reference new arguments to the logo block on the base Magento theme module. When seeking punctual change, it is highly recommended to use the **extend** technique.

When the changes are much deeper both in layout behavior and parameters, it is recommended to adopt the **override** technique.

To add an override, it is necessary to create a new directory in the root of your theme:

```
<theme_dir>/
---<Vendor>_<Module>/
------layout/
---------override/
------------base/
---------------layout.xml
```

The previous example shows how you can create a directory structure to override the Magento theme based on the configuration file.

For more information about override, access the official documentation `http://devdocs.magento.com/guides/v2.0/frontend-dev-guide/layouts/layout-override.html`.

Layout customizations

There are layout customization tasks that are the most common when developing themes and adjusting layouts, either for displaying the modules that are exhibited for users of the store or to the Magento administrative area.

Let's apply some of these customization tasks in the Bookstore theme.

Set the page layout

It's time to apply some more improvements on the Bookstore theme using the configuration techniques for customization in the layout layer.

To start the settings, go to the home page of your local instance of Magento 2 (`http://localhost/packt/`) and browse any product page as per the following example:

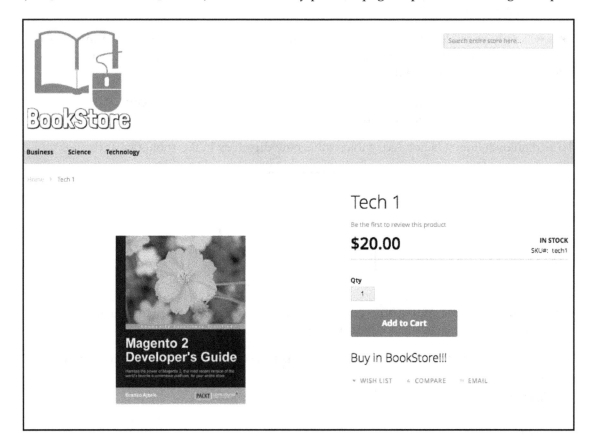

At this point we have a defined layout with only one main column, as you can see in the previous screenshot, but if you add a second column in the main content area of the website to exhibit related products, product comparison, and even customized blocks, you will change the page layout.

By default, the Magento layout has three ways to view the main content of the page in columns that are:

- One column
- Two columns left
- Two columns right
- Three columns

To change the visualization products page layout, do the following:

1. Open your favorite code editor.
2. Create the file `catalog_product_view.xml` and save it in the directory `app/design/frontend/Packt/bookstore/Magento_Catalog/layout`.
3. Add the following XML code in your file:

```
<?xml version="1.0"?>
<page layout="2columns-left"
xmlns:xsi="http://www.w3.org/2001/XMLSchema-    instance"
xsi:noNamespaceSchemaLocation="urn:magento:framework:View/Layout/etc/page_c
onfiguration.xsd">
    <body>
    <move element="product.info.stock.sku"
destination="product.info.price"  after="product.price.final"/>
    <move element="product.info.review" destination="product.info.main"
before="product.info.price"/>
    </body>
```

4. Open your terminal or Command Prompt, in the root directory of your Magento instance and run `php bin/magento cache:clean` to clear the cache.

Access the page to check the result:

Using the parameter `layout="2columns-left"`, in the file that controls the display of the layout of the product page, it was possible to change the behavior and consequently to render the content. The product page now has a column on the left side with two blocks, which are declared in other layout files, extending the functionalities and the user's navigation experience.

The `catalog_product_view.xml` file is part of the default declaration Magento system, but using the extend technique has changed the default behavior of its theme.

Remember that the Bookstore theme inherits Luma and Blank features.

Managing static resources

In the layout files it is also possible to add external resources such as CSS and JavaScript files to extend the functionality of your theme. Let's improve the Bookstore theme by adding a Google Fonts source for the page titles and menu text with the following steps:

1. Open your favorite code editor.
2. Create the `default_head_blocks.xml` file and save in the directory `Packt/bookstore/Magento_Theme/layout`.
3. Add the following XML code in the file:

```
<page xmlns:xsi="http://www.w3.org/2001/XMLSchema-instance"
xsi:noNamespaceSchemaLocation="urn:magento:framework:View/Layout/etc/page_c
onfigu ration.xsd">
    <head>
    <link src="https://fonts.googleapis.com/css?family=Pacifico"
src_type="url"    />\</head>
    </page>
```

4. Open the terminal or command prompt in the root directory of your Magento instance and clear the cache with the `php bin/magento cache:clean` command.
5. Still in the terminal or command prompt, run the grunt watch change monitor.
6. Open the file `Packt/bookstore/web/css/source/_theme.less` and insert at the end of the file the instruction: `h1, .ui-menu-item{font-family: 'Pacifico', cursive;}`.

Make sure that your Grunt task runner is working properly.

Reload your website to see the changes:

The `Pacifico` font was applied on the `<h1>` tags and menu items, as can be seen in the preceding screenshot. The `default_head_blocks.xml` file declares the use of the `Pacifico` font using the extend technique of Magento 2, making it possible to add more external files besides the files already declared in `default_head_blocks.xml`.

After the extension of the layout configuration file, simply add the CSS in the LESS file. Pretty simple isn't it?

Would you like to try new sources? Access the official Google Fonts website: `https://www.google.com/fonts`

Create a new test now. Let's say you no longer want to work with the `styles-m.css` file. You can remove this feature with the following instruction in the `default_head_blocks.xml` file:

```
<page xmlns:xsi="http://www.w3.org/2001/XMLSchema-instance"
xsi:noNamespaceSchemaLocation="urn:magento:framework:View/Layout/etc/page_c
onfiguration.xsd">
    <head>
      <link src="https://fonts.googleapis.com/css?family=Pacifico"
src_type="url" />
      <remove src="css/styles-m.css" />
    </head>
</page>
```

Clear the Magento cache and reload the page to see the result:

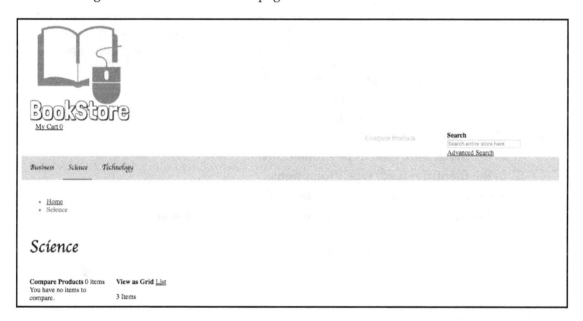

Like this you can manage all existing resources in your theme, as well as add new functionalities in removing CSS and JS files that runs by default in Magento 2. In previous examples, these adjustments are being applied on a global scope; however, you have the flexibility to add these instructions in specific layout configuration files of Magento modules.

Don't forget to return the `styles-m.css` file in Bookstore theme removing the instruction `<remove src="css/styles-m.css"/>`.

Working with static blocks

Magento 2 allows you to create static blocks and refer to them using the Magento admin area by creating blocks and widgets. Taking advantage of the two columns left of the product view page, add a new promotion block according to the following guidelines:

1. Access the Magento administrative area: `http://localhost/packt/admin_packt`.
2. Navigate to **Content** | **Blocks**.
3. Click on the **Add New Block** button.
4. In the **Block Title** field, type **Promotions**.
5. In the **Identifier** field, type **Promotions**.
6. Select **All Store Views** as the scope of display.
7. In **Content,** insert a title and three images with the same size that adjusts in the space on the left.
8. Click on the **Save Block** button.

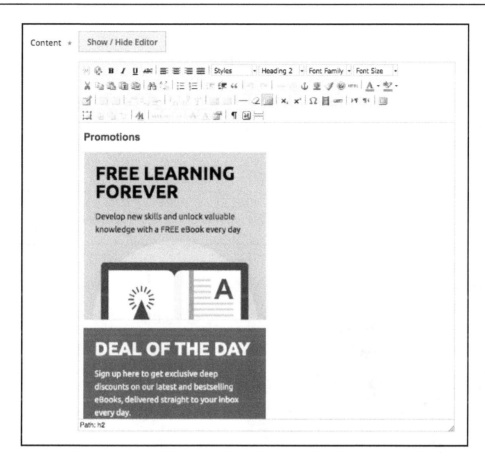

Once a block is created, it's time to insert it on the products visualization page, to do this, follow these steps:

1. In the administrative area, navigate to **Content | Widgets**.
2. Click on the **Add New Widget** button.
3. Choose as **Type: CMS Static Block**.
4. Choose as **Design Package: Bookstore** theme.
5. Type in the field **Widget Title: Promotions**.
6. In the **Layout Updates** block, click on the **Add Layout Update** button.
7. Select the **Specified Page** option in **Display On**.
8. Select the **Catalog Product View** in **Page**.
9. Select **Sidebar Main** as **Container**.
10. In the internal menu, navigate to **Widget** and select the block **Promotions**.
11. Save the widget and clear the cache.

Take a look at the following screenshot:

After these adjustments, reload the products visualization page to check the result:

Working with dynamic blocks

It is possible to work with blocks that have more access to dynamic parts of the Magento 2 system, such as a database and even a certain level of information processed. To do this, simply create blocks in your modules so you can use them in their containers.

In the next example, you will create a module called `Promo`, which will have a block and reference to a container to use in your theme. Do not worry so much now about backend development. The main idea is to explore options that the Magento system can offer to you.

Create the following directory structure for the new module:

- `<magento_root>/app/code/Packt/Promo`
- `<magento_root>/app/code/Packt/Promo/Block`
- `<magento_root>/app/code/Packt/Promo/etc`
- `<magento_root>/app/code/Packt/Promo/view`
- `<magento_root>/app/code/Packt/Promo/view/frontend`
- `<magento_root>/app/code/Packt/Promo/view/frontend/layout`
- `<magento_root>/app/code/Packt/Promo/view/frontend/templates`

For all modules in Magento 2, it is necessary to register it in the system. To register the module, create the file `<magento_root>/app/code/Packt/Promo/registration.php`:

```php
<?php
\Magento\Framework\Component\ComponentRegistrar::register(
    \Magento\Framework\Component\ComponentRegistrar::MODULE,
    'Packt_Promo',
    __DIR__
);
```

Now declare the `module.xml` file in the `<magento_root>/app/code/Packt/Promo/etc` directory:

```xml
<?xml version="1.0"?>
<config xmlns:xsi="http://www.w3.org/2001/XMLSchema-instance"
xsi:noNamespaceSchemaLocation="../../../../../lib/internal/Magento/Framewor
k/Module/etc/module.xsd">
    <module name="Packt_Promo" setup_version="0.0.0">
    </module>
</config>
```

Open your terminal or command prompt and run the `php bin/magento setup:upgrade` command to activate your new module:

```
Module 'Magento_TaxImportExport';
Module 'Magento_TaxSampleData';
Module 'Magento_GoogleAdwords';
Module 'Magento_CmsSampleData';
Module 'Magento_Translation';
Module 'Magento_Shipping';
Module 'Magento_Ups';
Module 'Magento_UrlRewrite';
Module 'Magento_CatalogRuleSampleData';
Module 'Magento_Usps';
Module 'Magento_Variable';
Module 'Magento_Version';
Module 'Magento_Webapi';
Module 'Magento_WebapiSecurity';
Module 'Magento_SalesRuleSampleData';
Module 'Magento_CatalogWidget';
Module 'Magento_WidgetSampleData';
Module 'Magento_Wishlist';
Module 'Magento_WishlistSampleData';
Module 'Packt_Promo';
Please re-run Magento compile command
SunnyGo:magento2 fjmiguel$
```

Now we'll create the block that will feed the template with the simple return of the block title. Create the file `<magento_root>/app/code/Packt/Promo/Block/Promo.php`:

```php
<?php
namespace Packt\Promo\Block;

/**
 * Promo block
 */
class Promo
    extends \Magento\Framework\View\Element\Template
{
    public function getTitle()
    {
        return "My Promotions Block";
    }
}
```

The new Promo block will be displayed on the main page. For this, we will extend the configuration file layout responsible for feeding the home page. Create the file `<magento_root>/app/code/Packt/Promo/view/frontend/layout/cms_index_index.xml`:

```xml
<?xml version="1.0"?>
<page xmlns:xsi="http://www.w3.org/2001/XMLSchema-instance"
xsi:noNamespaceSchemaLocation="../../../../../../../lib/internal/Magento/Framework/View/Layout/etc/page_configuration.xsd">
    <body>
        <referenceContainer name="main">
            <block class="Packt\Promo\Block\Promo" template="promo.phtml"/>
        </referenceContainer>
    </body>
</page>
```

Note that a reference to the main container for positioning the new layout is being made. `Packt\Promo\Block\Promo` is being declared, which is the block class responsible for sending messages to the `promo.phtml` template.

Create the `<magento_root>/app/code/Packt/Promo/view/frontend/templates/promo.phtml` file:

```php
<?php
/**
 * Promo view template
 *
 * @var $block Packt\Promo\Block\Promo
 */
?>
<h1 style="text-align:center;"><?php echo $block->getTitle(); ?></h1>
```

By creating the `$block` object and providing the `getTitle()` method declared in the class that contains the block, it is possible to directly manipulate the messages of Magento 2 and display them to the user in the website frontend.

Run `php bin/magento cache:clean` to clear the system cache and access the homepage of the website to see the results:

As a good practice, explore the modules layout files available in the `app/code` or `vendor/magento` directories to understand the dynamics of functioning and interaction between the modules and the core of Magento 2.

> For more information on how to manipulate elements in configuration layout, access the Magento official documentation at: `http://devdocs.magento.com/guides/v2.0/frontend-dev-guide/layouts/xml-manage.html`

Customizing templates

Besides the layout files manipulation to the positioning of elements on the page, according to the containers reference, it is also possible to implement improvements in the templates for your new theme with the techniques taught in this book.

At this point, I believe that the communication between the different elements of Magento 2 is clear and I am sure you will have many ideas for your projects using the techniques in the best possible way.

Besides the behavior customization of rendered pages via layout and your behavior via templates, it is also possible to customize the language of your store as a whole with the **Translation Dictionaries**.

In the next section, we will work on customization and theme translation.

Customizing templates with a new language

By default, Magento 2 works with a dictionary of words commonly used in the system, such as wishlist, view order, and print order. When working with a theme that will give support for more than one language, it is highly recommended to create a dictionary for each distinct translation.

Besides the template customization, you can customize strings for each language, extending the theme functionalities that are being developed. It is even possible to create your own language package for specific projects.

The default that Magento understands, the application of a given string in a template, is: `__('<your_string>')`.

For example, take a look at this code fragment of the **Add to Cart** button:

```
<div class="actions">
<button type="submit"

        class="action primary tocart"
id="product-addtocart-button">
<span><?php echo __('Add to Cart') ?></span>
</button>
</div>
```

For all language dictionaries that contain the phrase *Add to Cart*, it will be automatically assigned to the template according to the user's selected language.

For more information about customizing strings, access the official documentation at `http://devdocs.magento.com/guides/v2.0/frontend -dev-guide/translations/translate_theory.html`.

In the exercise on the Bookstore theme, the addition of the German language will be simulated as well as the English language that is set as default in the theme.

For managing languages, Magento 2 adopted the pattern of **i18n** internationalization content availability. This pattern facilitates and organizes the product development process in different languages. All the directories that relate to this pattern are named i18n to standardize this layer.

To create the pattern structure of translation on the Bookstore theme:

1. Create the directory
   `<magento_root>/app/design/frontend/Packt/bookstore/i18n`.

2. In the i18n directory, create the files `de_DE.csv` e `en_US.csv`.

3. Open the terminal or command prompt and run the following commands:

```
    php bin/magento i18n:collect-phrases--
output="app/design/frontend/Packt/bookstore/i18n/en_US.csv"
app/design/frontend/Packt/bookstore
    php bin/magento i18n:collect-phrases--
output="app/design/frontend/Packt/bookstore/i18n/de_DE.csv"
app/design/frontend/Packt/bookstore
```

The commands used in the Magento CLI tool allow you to create a basic CSV file with the strings that can be translated, which greatly facilitates the work of the theme developer.

 For more information about the Magento CLI tool command, access the official documentation available at: `http://devdocs.magento.com/guide s/v2.0/config-guide/cli/config-cli-subcommands-i18n.html`.

If all goes well, you will have the following directory in your Bookstore theme:

Open the de_DE.csv file and put your German translation theme, as shown in the following example:

```
"Shop By","Einkaufen nach"
"Shopping Options","Einkaufsoptionen"
"Category","Kategorie"
"Compare Products","Produkte vergleichen"
"Print This Page","Drucke diese Seite"
"Remove Product","Entfernen artikel"
"Product","Produkt"
"Add to Cart","Warenkorb legen"
"In stock","Auf Lager"
"Out of stock","Ausverkauft"
"Add to Wish List","Wunschliste"
"You have no items to compare.","Sie haben keine Produkte zum Vergleich."
"Remove This Item","Entfernen Sie diesen Artikel"
"Compare","Vergleichen"
"Clear All","Alles löschen"
"Close Window","Fenster schliessen"
```

Remembering that the CSV structure must be maintained with the phrase/left word being the default string and the phrase/right word being the translation. Make a test with other languages. You can even customize the en_US language and also create dictionaries for specific modules.

Now it will be necessary to activate a second **Store View** in the Magento administrative area. This **Store View** will be configured to the **German** language:

1. Login to the administrative area: `http://localhost/packt/admin_packt`.
2. Access the menu **Stores** | **All Stores**.
3. Click on the **Create Store View** button.
4. Configure the new **Store View** so that it has the new language as the image:

5. Save the **Store View**.

Once the **Store View** is saved you need to inform the Magento system of which language will be used by the new **Store View**:

1. Navigate to the menu **Stores** | **Configuration**.
2. In the drop-down box on top of **Stores Configuration,** select the **German** view.
3. Access the **General** submenu and in the **Locale Options** block select **German (Germany)** as the option.
4. Save the settings.

Because you have one theme with two translations, Grunt task runner should monitor one more theme scope. So it is necessary to declare this change in the `<magento_root>/dev/tools/grunt/configs/themes.js` configuration file by changing the following statement:

```
bookstore: {
        area: 'frontend',
        name: 'Packt/bookstore',
        locale: 'en_US',
        files: [
            'css/styles-m',
            'css/styles-l'
        ],
        dsl: 'less'
    },
```

To the following:

```
bookstore_en_US: {
area: 'frontend',
    name: 'Packt/bookstore',
    locale: 'en_US',
    files: [
            'css/styles-m',
            'css/styles-l',
            'mage/gallery/gallery',
            'css/print'
    ],
    dsl: 'less'
},

bookstore_de_DE: {
area: 'frontend',
```

```
    name: 'Packt/bookstore',
  locale: 'de_DE',
   files: [
           'css/styles-m',
           'css/styles-l',
           'mage/gallery/gallery',
           'css/print'
   ],
  dsl: 'less'
},
```

After saving the themes configuration file it is necessary to make a new deployment of the theme structure so that your themes work with two distinct languages with integration to Grunt:

1. Remove directories `var/cache`, `var/pub/static` and `var/view_processed`.
2. Run `php bin/magento setup: static-content:deploy en_US de_DE` to make the new deployment for two languages.
3. Run the command `grunt exec:bookstore_en_US`.
4. Run the command `grunt exec:bookstore_de_DE`.
5. Run the command `grunt less:bookstore_en_US`.
6. Run the command `grunt less:bookstore_de_DE`.
7. If the static files were unavailable after this process, repeat the command `php bin/magento setup:static-content:deploy`.

After this, you must generate new indexing in Magento. To do this, run the command `php bin/magento indexer:reindex` on the terminal or command prompt.

Access the homepage of your local Magento instance and you will find a new available menu on the top on the right side with the **Default Store View** text. Click on the menu and select the **German** language.

> Default welcome msg! Sign In or Create an Account   German

Access the product view page to check the customization that was applied to the templates and languages level:

For more information about translations at Magento 2, access the official documentation at `http://devdocs.magento.com/guides/v2.0/frontend -dev-guide/translations/xlate.html`.

Summary

In the previous chapters, you obtained a basic understanding of the functioning of scheme layouts. In this chapter, it was possible to strengthen this concept and understand the correct manipulation, customization, and configuration of layouts files for developing themes and customization of Magento modules.

In the next chapter, the JavaScript concepts will be applied in the Bookstore theme development.

9
Magento 2 JavaScript

"The only place success comes before work is in the dictionary." – Vince Lombardi.

Magento 2 adopted a complete framework for JavaScript solutions in order to provide greater performance and uncoupling modules aiming for higher reusability of codes.

Good practice and current techniques were also employed with the objective of facilitating the development of solutions in the infrastructure that Magento 2 provides both to its users and to its developers.

In this chapter, we will cover:

- Magento 2 JavaScript structure
- Initializing and locating JavaScript component
- Magento jQuery widgets
- Creating a jCarousel component for the Promo module

Magento 2 JavaScript structure

The use of JavaScript in web application projects has evolved in recent years because of the functionalities, facilities, and portability that this technology provides to users.

The inclusion of the JavaScript files was made exclusively through insertion in the page headers, which has caused a big problem in performance and page loading.

In previous versions of Magento it was discussed in relation to good practice using the JavaScript and standardization of use of libraries, such as **jQuery** (http://jquery.com/) and **Prototype** (http://prototypejs.org/). In order to provide greater management power and performance of JavaScript, Magento 2 uses **RequireJS** (http://requirejs.org /) as a standard to load JavaScript libraries.

RequireJS is a JavaScript file and module loader and it implements the standard and **Asynchronous Module Definition (AMD)**. This type of pattern allows JavaScript to run without it to be declared in a global scope, such as layout configuration files and allows a same single file and/or JavaScript library to be shared between distinct system modules.

Another feature of RequireJS is to be lazy loaded, so that it does not load any module unless there is a dependency of module use in the page being loaded.

Following this notation, JavaScript can be used in Magento 2 as:

- **JavaScript component**: Can be any .js with the use of the AMD technique
- **UI component**: Component located on the Magento_Ui module on the directory app/code/Magento/Ui/view
- **jQuery e jQuery UI widgets**: jQuery and jQuery UI components used on Magento 2 to create widgets

In the next section, the use of the RequireJS techniques will be presented as well as practical examples to use in the development of your themes.

Initializing and locating JavaScript component

With the portability provided by RequireJS, you can specify JavaScript resources used in your modules and themes. The scope of action, as well as the basic structure of directories can be defined in:

- **Library**: JavaScript libraries used for application of libraries and archives in several modules and themes, aiming at the reuse in themes projects. Addresses the use in the `lib/web` directory.
- **Module**: Application of libraries and files with the reduced scope, acting only in the module. Addresses its use in the `<module_dir>/view/<areaname>/web`.
- **Theme**: Application of libraries and archives with reduced scope, acting only in the theme. Addresses its use in the directory `<theme_dir>/<VendorName>_<ModuleName>/web`.

> For more information about JavaScript resources on Magento 2, access the official documentation available at `http://devdocs.magento.com/guides` `/v2.1/javascript-dev-guide/javascript/js-resources.html`.

Initializing JavaScript

It is highly recommended as good practice to declare the JavaScript resources in the templates instead of layouts updates, mainly to take advantage of the processing and loading via RequireJS.

There are two ways to initialize a JavaScript component on the templates:

Imperative Initialization and **Declarative Initialization**. On the imperative initialization, Magento 2 allows raw code to be used and applied to the business layer as well as to work in two ways using the JavaScript resources on your template files with the IDs notation: RequireJS ID e Magento Modulate ID.

See the following example of declaration using RequireJS ID:

```
require(["jquery"], function($){
   /*my code here*/
});
```

With this call it is possible to load the jQuery library to the function in the template, creating a widget of your theme or module development. You will see in the following sequence that it is possible to map these dependencies to facilitate the use of JavaScript components.

Now see an example of the declaration using Magento Modulate ID:

```
require(["Magento_Sales/order/create/form"], function(){
    /*my code here*/
});
```

In the preceding example, the file `form.js` is loaded into a determined template through the reference `Magento_Sales/order/create/form`. With this type of reference, it is possible to reuse the resources in different templates.

The declarative initialization allows for the preparation of all the backend layer to the response that has been sent to a page source using standard tools. There are also two ways to work with declarative initialization:

- Using the attribute, `data-mage-init`
- Using the tag, `<script type="text/x-magento-init"/>`

The `data-mage-int` can be used inside the tags. Here is an example of initialization in the `<nav>` tag:

```
<nav data-mage-init='{ "<component_name>": {...} }'></nav>
```

Using the tag `<script type="text/x-magento-init">`, the HTML will not have direct access to the element. See the following example:

```
<script type="text/x-magento-init">
{
    "#main-container": {
        "navigation": <?php echo $block->getNavigationConfig(); ?>,
        "accordion": <?php echo $block->getNavigationAccordionConfig(); ?>
    },
    "*": {
        "pageCache": <?php echo $block->getPageCacheConfig(); ?>
    }
}
</script>
```

You can use the declarative way for the passage of backend parameters, once everything has been processed on the server-side before delivering the response in the template.

The use of the two approaches depends on the scope of the project to which you are working.

For more information about ways of initialization, access the official documentation at `http://devdocs.magento.com/guides/v2.1/javascri pt-dev-guide/javascript/js_init.html`.

Mapping the JavaScript resources

With the objective to facilitate the declaration of dependencies in RequireJS, it is possible to create aliases to the files and JavaScript libraries. For this task, Magento works with a standard file called `requires-config.js`. The `requires-config.js` file can act at different levels according to the scope of action. For example, the mapping of JavaScript resources used in the native Catalog module is available in the path `app/code/Magento/Catalog/view/frontend/requirejs-config.js`, as:

```
var config = {
    "paths": {
                "product": "./product/product"
    }
};
```

All the modules and themes in the Magento 2 system may have the `requirejs-config.js` file as a reference to the used libraries. The configuration file always uses the relative path according to the directory. By default, this file is inserted in the directory view/frontend of the modules and themes.

To reference third-party libraries in the `requirejs-config.js` configuration file, you can use the `shim` instruction:

```
var config = {
  "paths": {
                "product": "./product/product"
      },
  "shim": {
     "3-rd-party-plugin": ["jquery"]
  }
};
```

If there are different versions of your file or you want more options for a mapping of various resources, you can also use the `map` instruction:

```
var config = {
  map":{
          "*":{
              "product": "./product/product"
```

```
        }
      },
  "shim": {
    "3-rd-party-plugin": ["jquery"]
  }
};
```

> For more information about map, access the RequireJS documentation at h
> ttp://requirejs.org/docs/api.html#config-map.

Magento jQuery widgets

In version 2 of Magento, it adopted the use of the jQuery library as the main JavaScript library. Also, with the adoption of RequireJS, the use of jQuery has become modular and provides easy management between the different layers of visualization and templates enabling the creation of widgets.

Besides jQuery, jQuery UI can also be used for your projects with the same idea of creating widgets. Currently, Magento 2 supports jQuery UI 1.9.2 version with a peculiarity: the style sheet files are added separately to avoid problems with the existing Magento 2 stylesheet files.

The main jQuery widgets that can be used on Magento are:

- Accordion widget
- Alert widget
- Calendar widget
- Collapsible widget
- Confirm widget
- Dropdown Dialog widget
- Gallery widget
- List widget
- Loader widget
- Menu widget
- Modal widget
- Navigation widget
- Prompt widget

- QuickSearch widget
- Tabs widget

They all follow the functionalities of the jQuery library and can be applied in the Magento templates. You can test them and consult the documentation, available for the collection of ideas, but to exemplify the use of jQuery widgets in your Magento themes projects, we will demonstrate a method to customize the Bookstore theme.

 For more information about jQuery widgets on Magento 2, access the official documentation available at `http://devdocs.magento.com/guides /v2.1/javascript-dev-guide/widgets/jquery-widgets-about.html`.

Creating a Tabs widget

To practice the techniques seen so far, you will implement a Tabs widget in the product view page. This widget will be a mini FAQ with information about the shopping process in the store.

First copy the file `/vendor/magento/module-catalog/view/frontend/templates/product/view/details.phtml` to the directory `/app/design/frontend/Packt/bookstore/Magento_Catalog/templates/product/view`.

Open the file on your favorite code editor and at the end of the file add the following markup:

```
<h2>FAQ</h2>
<div id="tabs">
  <ul>
    <li><a href="#tabs-1">How can I download eBooks?</a></li>
    <li><a href="#tabs-2">What payment methods can I use?</a></li>
    <li><a href="#tabs-3">What format are Bookstore eBooks?</a></li>
  </ul>
  <div id="tabs-1">
    <p>Once you complete your eBook purchase, the download link for your
eBook will be available in your account.</p>
  </div>
  <div id="tabs-2">
    <p>You can pay with the following card types:
      <ol>
        <li>Visa Debit</li>
        <li>Visa Credit</li>
        <li>MasterCard</li>
```

```
          <li>PayPal</li>
          <li>American Express</li>
       </ol>
    </p>
  </div>
  <div id="tabs-3">
     <p>Bookstore eBooks can be downloaded as a PDF, EPUB or MOBI file. They
can also be viewed online.</p>
  </div>
</div>

<script>
require(['jquery','jquery/ui'],function($, tabs) {
  $("#tabs").tabs();
});
</script>
```

The first part is an HTML code that will contain the content of your tabs. From the
`<script>` element, the `require` function is used to load the jQuery and jQuery UI libraries.
At the end, the instruction `$ ("# tabs").tabs( )` runs the script and applies the **Tabs**
widget.

Do you remember that the Magento default does not contain the jQuery UI CSS file? It will
be necessary to generate customized library contents on the website of jQuery UI (`http://j
queryui.com/download/`) and select only the following options:

- **Version**: 1.9.2
- **UI Core**: Core, Widget
- **Widgets**: Tabs

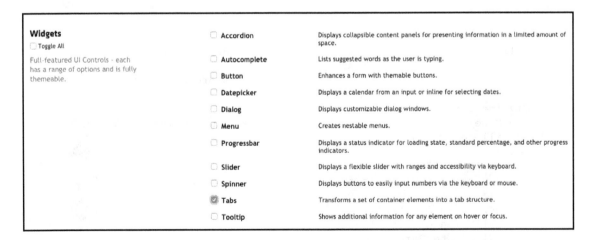

After selecting the options, download the file and extract it in a directory. Rename the file `jquery-ui1.9.2.custom.min.css` to `jquery-ui1.9.2.custom.min.less` and copy it to the directory `/app/design/frontend/Packt/bookstore/Magento_Catalog/web/css/source/`.

Open the file `/app/design/frontend/Packt/bookstore/Magento_Catalog/web/css/source/_module.less`, that was used in **Chapter 5**, *Creating a Responsive Magento 2 Theme*, and add the following instruction at the beginning of the file:

```
@import 'jquery-ui-1.9.2.custom.min.less';
```

This instruction will do the import of the file to the LESS processing in the `Magento_Catalog` module.

Now do the following process to update the system and apply the updates:

1. Open the terminal or Command Prompt and access the root directory in your Magento 2 instance.
2. Run the commands `grunt exec:bookstore_en_US` and `grunt exec:bookstore_de_DE`.
3. Run the commands `grunt less:bookstore_en_US` and `grunt less:bookstore_de_DE`.
4. Run the commands `php bin/magento setup:static-content:deploy en_US` and `php bin/magento setup:static-content:deploy de_DE`.
5. Lastly, run the command `php bin/magento cache:clean`.

Open the visualization page at some product to see the result:

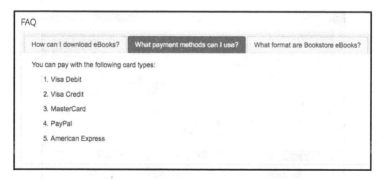

Very simple, isn't it?

Now, what if you want to add your own script to `requirejs` or even insert an external script or another library plugin in your theme development project, and what if you wanted this new script that has already received data and been integrated directly with the Magento 2 database?

In the following section of this chapter, you will make a new implementation using the techniques learned here. This time, RequireJS in the Promo module will be implemented, which is developed in `Chapter 8`, *Magento Layout Development*, using a jQuery plugin and an integration with the products system.

Creating a jCarousel component for Promo module

The final objective of this practice is that you have the Promo module functioning on the main page of your Bookstore theme integrated with `jCarousel` and displaying images of registered products in the administrative area of Magento. They will be integrated into different layers to show a unique result in your theme.

For this practice, you will use the responsive carousel feature provided by the `jCarousel` plugin (`http://sorgalla.com/jcarousel/`), which serves as a vertical and horizontal control for item lists in HTML. This excellent plugin was created by Jan Sorgalla and has long been used by developers in frontend projects with jQuery.

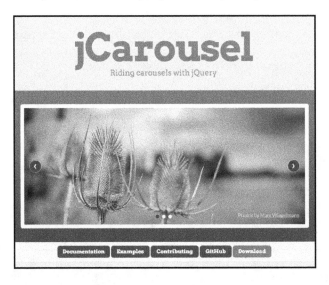

Beginning the implementation, access the download page of the jCarousel plugin and download the following JavaScript files:

- jCarousel Core – Production Version
- Control Plugin – Production Version
- Pagination Plugin – Production Version

Move these files to the directory `/app/code/Packt/Promo/view/frontend/web/js`.

Download the file `http://sorgalla.com/jcarousel/examples/responsive/jcarousel.responsive.css`, rename it to `jcarousel.responsive.less`, and save it in the directory `/app/code/Packt/Promo/view/frontend/web/css`.

Once you have the jCarousel library available, it's time to create references to the functioning in the module. First, create the `requirejs-config.js` file in the directory `/app/code/Packt/Promo/view/frontend/` and insert the following code:

```
var config = {
    "map":{
        "*":{
            promo: "Packt_Promo/js/promo"
        }
    },

    "shim": {
      "Packt_Promo/js/jquery.jcarousel-core.min": ["jquery"],
      "Packt_Promo/js/jquery.jcarousel-control.min": ["jquery"],
      "Packt_Promo/js/jquery.jcarousel-pagination.min": ["jquery"]
    }
};
```

In the configuration file `promo: "Packt_Promo/js/promo"` has been mapped, that is a custom JavaScript called `promo.js`, which will be created in the next sequence, as well as the referenced dependencies by the parameter `"shim"`. These external dependencies refer to the jCarousel library that is being used in the project.

Now create the `promo.js` file in the directory `/app/code/Packt/Promo/view/frontend/web/js` with the following codification:

```
define([
   'jquery',
   'Packt_Promo/js/jquery.jcarousel-core.min',
   'Packt_Promo/js/jquery.jcarousel-control.min',
   'Packt_Promo/js/jquery.jcarousel-pagination.min'
], function($){
```

```
        var o = {};

    o.promoBlock = function(jcarousel, prev, next, pagination){
      var jcarousel = $(jcarousel);
        jcarousel
            .on('jcarousel:reload jcarousel:create', function () {
                var carousel = $(this),
                    width = carousel.innerWidth();

                if (width >= 600) {
                    width = width / 3;
                } else if (width >= 350) {
                    width = width / 2;
                }

                carousel.jcarousel('items').css('width', Math.ceil(width) +
'px');
            })
            .jcarousel({
                wrap: 'circular'
            });

        $(prev)
            .jcarouselControl({
                target: '-=1'
            });

        $(next)
            .jcarouselControl({
                target: '+=1'
            });

        $(pagination)
            .on('jcarouselpagination:active', 'a', function() {
                $(this).addClass('active');
            })
            .on('jcarouselpagination:inactive', 'a', function() {
                $(this).removeClass('active');
            })
            .on('click', function(e) {
                e.preventDefault();
            })
            .jcarouselPagination({
                perPage: 1,
                item: function(page) {
                    return '<a href="#' + page + '">' + page + '</a>';
                }
            });
```

```
    }

    return o;
  });
```

The custom JavaScript called `promo.js`, aims to carry the functionalities of control and pagination of the jCarousel plugin to be available for use in the template.

In the instruction definition, the external files are loaded to be used in custom JavaScript. In the second parameter of the function, `define` has already created the object o and has declared a method called `o.promoBlock()`. In the `promoBlock()` method that receives the template parameters to the jCarousel configuration, the jCarousel functionalities are declared that interact with the size of the images and the dynamic change of HTML and CSS files to create the effect/animation of the image carousel.

It is important at this point to note that JavaScript works with `callback` functions or `higher-order` functions; that is, basically, it is possible to pass a function as a parameter to another function. This book does not have the scope of deepening the JavaScript techniques, but it is strongly recommended that you improve your studies by researching it further.

Open the layout configuration file `/app/code/Packt/Promo/view/frontend/layout/cms_index_index.xml` and add the following code on line 3:

```
<head>
<css src="Packt_Promo::css/jcarousel.responsive.css"/>
</head>
```

This code will be responsible for loading the jCarousel styles file in the `Promo` module.

At this point, you should have the following directories and file structure:

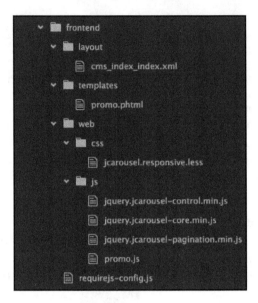

Now that you've included in the jCarousel module the already made declaration of the JavaScript file configuration and execution and have also declared the CSS file, it's time to focus on the module's objective. To begin the integration with products registered in the administrative area, open the file /app/code/Packt/Promo/Block/Promo.php and enter the following code:

```php
<?php
namespace Packt\Promo\Block;

/**
 * Promo block
 */
class Promo
    extends \Magento\Framework\View\Element\Template{

    protected $context;
    protected $_categoryFactory;
    protected $storeManager;

    public function __construct(
    \Magento\Backend\Block\Template\Context $context,
    \Magento\Catalog\Model\CategoryFactory $categoryFactory,
    \Magento\Store\Model\StoreManagerInterface $storeManager,
    array $data = []
    ){
```

```
        $this->_storeManager=$storeManager;
        $this->_categoryFactory = $categoryFactory;
        parent::__construct($context, $data);
    }

    public function getCategory($categoryId){
        $category = $this->_categoryFactory->create();
        $category->load($categoryId);
        return $category;
    }

    public function getCategoryProducts($categoryId){
        $products = $this->getCategory($categoryId)->getProductCollection();
        $products->addAttributeToSelect('small_image');
        return $products;
    }

    public function getProductUrlImage(){
        return
$this->_storeManager->getStore()->getBaseUrl(\Magento\Framework\UrlInterfac
e::URL_TYPE_MEDIA) .
        "catalog/product";
    }

    public function getTitle(){
        return "My Promotions Block";
    }
}
```

Initially, in the Promo class, there was only the getTitle() method that returns the module title. Now, besides the constructor method, three different methods were inserted that will be better detailed in the next section.

The constructor method injects three classes in the Promo class which can be highlighted CategoryFactory and StoreManagerInterface, and which provide methods for manipulating catalog information and the base URL of the store, respectively. At this point it is necessary to insert the parent::__construct referencing the $context, with the objective of being a container for other objects of a super class.

On the getCategory() method, the category searched by ID is returned. This method will be used in the template to reference the category of images of products to be displayed on the module using the object, $_categoryFactory.

With the selected category, it is possible to return the collection of products by the `getCategoryProducts()` method through the instruction `$this->getCategory ($categoryId)->getProductCollection()`, limiting the data return scope only to small product images through the instruction, `$products->addAttributeToSelect ('small_image')`.

The method `getProductUrlImage()` returns the store URL joining with the string `"catalog/product"` so that images can be displayed on jCarousel with your absolute URL, dynamically.

 For more information, access the official documentation for backend development of Magento 2 at `http://devdocs.magento.com/guides/v2. 1/extension-dev-guide/bk-extension-dev-guide.html`.

It only lacks the `promo.phtml` template to receive the implementation of jCarousel but first, enter the administrative area and access the **Products | Categories** menu. Create a new sub-category of products inside the **Default** category, called **Promotions**:

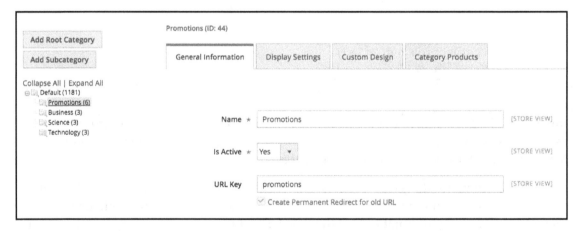

This category will be used to refer to the products in the Promo module. Do not forget, at the time of creation, to mark the option for the new subcategory to not be shown as a menu item:

After creation, take note of the ID number that will be generated by the system. You will need this number to configure the display `Promo` module template:

Add products to the **Promotions** category so that it has to take at least six registered products:

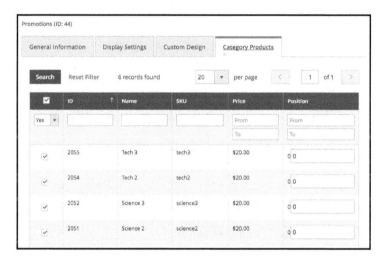

Be aware that the ID number can vary. Write down the number that is generated in your system for later use on the template `promo.phtml`.

Now open the file `/app/code/Packt/Promo/view/frontend/templates/promo.phtml` and insert the following code:

```php
<?php
/**
 * Promo view template
 *
 * @var $block PacktPromoBlockPromo
 */

$productCollection = $block->getCategoryProducts(YOUR_PROMOTIONS_ID);
$mediaUrl = $block->getProductUrlImage();

?>

<h1 style="text-align:center;"><?php echo $block->getTitle(); ?></h1>
```

```
<div class="wrapper">

        <div class="jcarousel-wrapper">
            <div class="jcarousel">
                <ul>
                  <?php
                    foreach ($productCollection as $product) {
                        echo '<li><img src="' .
                             $mediaUrl .
                             $product->getData()['small_image'] .
                             '" alt="Image 1"></li>';
                    }
                  ?>
                </ul>
            </div>

            <a href="#" class="jcarousel-control-prev">&lsaquo;</a>
            <a href="#" class="jcarousel-control-next">&rsaquo;</a>

            <p class="jcarousel-pagination"></p>
        </div>
    </div>
<script>
requirejs(['promo'], function(promo){
  promo.promoBlock('.jcarousel', '.jcarousel-control-prev', '.jcarousel-
control-next', '.jcarousel-pagination');
});
</script>
```

This template file has PHP instructions (backend), HTML, and JS (frontend) performing a complete integration of the Promo module.

The $productCollection variable receives the registered products of the Promotions category through $block-query>getCategoryProducts(), which is passed the subcategory ID to the method declaration in the Block/Promo class. The $mediaUrl variable receives the absolute URL of the product images. The entire HTML structure and the declaration of classes in each tag are structured according to the jCarousel documentation.

The code snippet is as follows:

```
<?php
foreach ($productCollection as $product) {
echo '<li><img src="' .
           $mediaUrl .
           $product->getData()['small_image'] .
           '" alt="Image 1"></li>';
```

```
}
?>
```

It is responsible for *writing* all the main images from the Promotions category, dynamically feeding the `<img>` tag and feeding the necessary listing for the `jCarousel` function according to the proposal.

Take a look at the following In the snippet:

```
<script>
requirejs(['promo'], function(promo){
   promo.promoBlock('.jcarousel', '.jcarousel-control-prev', '.jcarousel-
control-next', '.jcarousel-pagination');
});
</script>
```

It creates a reference to the custom JavaScript `promo.js` feeding the parameters required so that the file returns to the main function of jCarousel.

Perfect! You already have your module developed and functioning. However, it is still not ready to be installed in other Magento 2 instances because it does not have its declaration of the `composer.json` file. Create a `composer.json` file in the `/app/code/ Packt/Promo/` directory:

```
{
  "name": "packt/promo",
  "description": "Module that creates a new Promotion block",
  "type": "magento2-module",
  "version": "1.0.0",
  "license": [
    "OSL-3.0",
    "AFL-3.0"
  ],
  "require": {
    "php": "~5.5.0|~5.6.0|~7.0.0",
    "magento/framework": "~100.0.4"
  },
  "autoload": {
    "files": [ "registration.php" ],
    "psr-4": {
      "Packt\\Promo": ""
    }
  }
}
```

Do not worry for now about the meaning of this file. In the next chapter, we will approach its use in greater depth.

To finish the changes, carry out the following procedure:

1. Open the terminal or prompt command and access the root directory on your Magento 2 instance.
2. Run the commands `grunt exec:bookstore_en_US` and `grunt exec:bookstore_de_DE`.
3. Run the commands `grunt less:bookstore_en_US` and `grunt less:bookstore_de_DE`.
4. Run the commands `php bin/magento setup:static-content:deploy en_US` and `php bin/magento setup:static-content:deploy de_DE`.
5. Lastly, run the command `php bin/magento cache:clean`.

Reload the homepage of your Magento 2 instance to check the result:

Summary

In this chapter, you practiced enough to use the libraries and custom JavaScript files in the Magento system 2. It was also possible to understand the current techniques for modularization of JavaScript components using the RequireJS library, a library that was adopted to be used natively in the Magento 2 system.

It was possible to apply the techniques learned in two practical implementations at the level of customization of themes, creating a Tabs widget, and the level of customization modules by applying an integration between backend and frontend using jCarousel as custom JavaScript in the Promo module.

In the next chapter, we will create an integrated Magento 2 module for Twitter using the techniques learned so far.

10
Social Media in Magento 2

"I can't change the direction of the wind, but I can adjust my sails to always reach my destination". Jimmy Dean.

In this chapter you will learn more about Magento 2 module development. It is a big professional differential that you can create Magento 2 in increasingly customized solutions. The importance of knowing the different layers and interactions among the distinct components of Magento 2 will increasingly contribute to your improvement and especially to the quality you will deliver on your projects.

In the previous chapter, you used the jCarousel library to enrich your theme project. In this chapter you will make a direct integration with Twitter REST API.

The following topics will be covered in this chapter:

- Magento Components
- Development Workflow
- Developing the Sweet Tweet module

Magento components

Before starting the new project, it is important to know more about Magento 2 concepts. The professionals who have knowledge both in frontend development and backend development are valued professionals in the Information Technology market. With this convergence of knowledge on different Magento areas, you can provide more robust solutions on theme development even extending the functionalities and providing a greater level of customization for users and system administrators. It is important to understand the Magento mechanism or Magento components.

The Magento components can be listed as follows:

- **Themes**: Changes the layout disposition to the final user, both in the category colors as in the category functionalities in the user navigation (UX).
- **Modules**: Developed for a specific purpose. They can be used for user interaction or even to provide greater functionalities in the system.
- **Languages**: Allows you to translate your Magento system into different languages .

The modularity of the Magento system allows you to create unique solutions providing consequently greater flexibility. All the three layers of Magento components are worked in this book and you can get some experience with the same by applying concepts and techniques that could bring additional results by the study and development of Magento 2 solutions.

In the next section of the chapter you will be exploring the modules development layer further in order to get more experience and understanding of the components integration of Magento 2 system, as well as to improve the development of any future themes creating numerous possibilities.

Development workflow

The development of Magento 2 components follows the minimum criteria necessary so that it can achieve the goal of delivering a theme or a functional module to your user and/ or client. These criteria are listed as follows:

- Dependencies declaration via `composer.json`
- Component registration using `registration.php`
- Components definition via XML components
- Publication and distribution of developed components

The act of declaring a file `composer.json` is good practice for dependency management of components as well as containing important information about the theme or module that is being developed.

The `registration.php` file already allows the Magento system to make the registration of the new component that can be used in the scope that you intend, and it can be added to core components of Magento in order to reuse the code already produced.

For example, the declaration of XML definition files enables the nomenclature of your component as well as the versions parameterization.

After this minimum necessary process, you will be very close to distributing your new Magento 2 component.

Understanding the composer.json

In `Chapter 1`, *Introduction to Magento 2*, the Composer installation was made in your Operating System. At this point of studying Magento 2 theme development, its importance as a standard definition is evident. The use of Composer provides the following advantages:

- Use of third-party libraries in your projects in an organized and sustainable manner
- Robust architecture for component dependency management
- Reduction of compatibility of conflicts among extensions
- Semantic versioning dependencies
- Supports the PSR standards

> For more information about the Composer access the official documentation available on `https://getcomposer.org/doc/00-intro.md`.

The `composer.json` file allows your component to interact directly with the Composer dependency management system and mainly it is the locale where information related to your theme or module is declared.

See an example of a declaration of a file taken from the own `composer.json` file website `https://getcomposer.org/`:

```
{
    "repositories": [
        {
            "type": "git",
            "url": "https://github.com/foobar/intermediate.git"
        },
        {
            "type": "pear",
            "url": "http://pear.foobar.repo",
            "vendor-alias": "foobar"
        }
    ],
```

```
"require": {
    "foobar/TopLevelPackage1": "*",
    "foobar/TopLevelPackage2": "*"
  }
}
```

In this example, two distinct repositories are being declared to the component besides two packages that are required (dependencies) inside of your hypothetical component and/or module.

 For more information about the Composer integration with the Magento 2 access the documentation at `http://devdocs.magento.com/guides/v2.1 /extension-dev-guide/build/composer-integration.html`.

In the sequence, you will make an effective practical use application of the `composer.json` on the development of a Magento 2 module.

Developing the Sweet Tweet module

To go a little deeper on the concepts seen so far, we will develop a new module called **Sweet Tweet** integrating with social media. This module will make an integration with the **Application Programming Interface** (**API**) of Twitter and it will be used to display tweets with hashtags **#magento2**, **#magentodev** and **#magentolive** in the visualization layer of your Magento 2 instance. With this practice it will be possible to memorize even more the concept of componentization and managing dependencies via `composer.json` file.

In the previous development of the Promo module, you used the jCarousel library as a third-party library. In the development of the Sweet Tweet module you will use the **TwitterOAuth** authentication package that enables authentication on the API layer Twitter but with a crucial difference: You will use the `composer.json` to manage this additional package in a more effective way.

The Twitter REST API

The Twitter developers' area (`https://dev.twitter.com/`) provides documentation about its API so developers all over the world can create applications that have interaction directly with the Twitter database providing a series of options, parameterization and ways to exchange messages using the **Representational State Transfer** (**REST**) architecture. The REST API uses OAuth (`http://oauth.net/`) technology to identify Twitter applications. Users and its responses are available in JSON format.

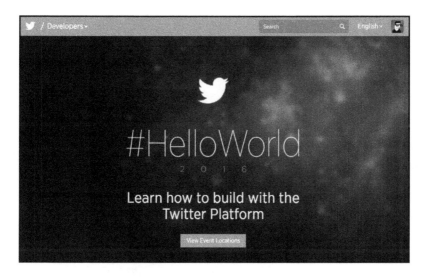

For the development of the new module, it will be necessary for you to have an activated account on Twitter to generate the access tokens that are responsible for the authentication of your application with the REST API Twitter.

Access the address `https://apps.twitter.com` and click on the **Create New App** button. You will have access to the creation page and fill in the following fields:

- **Name**: name of your application
- **Description**: description of your application
- **Website**: website that refers to your application

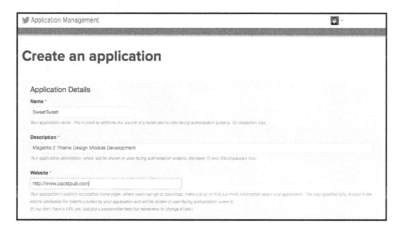

After accepting the Developer Agreement from Twitter click on the **Create your Twitter Application** button. Access the applications configuration by clicking on your new application and click on the **Keys** and **Access Tokens** tab to take note of the following fields:

- Consumer Key (API Key)
- Consumer Secret (API Secret)
- Access Token
- Access Token Secret

Keep these fields because they will be needed later in the solution development sequence.

> To learn more about the REST API options available on Twitter access the link `https://dev.twitter.com/rest/public`.

The Twitter OAuth library

The library Twitter OAuth (`https://twitteroauth.com/`) was created by Abraham Williams in order to provide a transparent way to authenticate applications with the REST API Twitter. Well used by the development community, this library will be used as a third-party library to develop the Sweet Tweet module.

In addition, to provide the OAuth authentication method, the library provides the methods of `GET`, `POST`, `Proxy`, and others that complement a robust solution for those who want to use this library in their application.

To use this library on the Sweet Tweet module, the process will be a little different from the usual. You will use the Composer and the `composer.json` file to install this dependency on the Sweet Tweet module in the nest section of the chapter.

> For more information about the Twitter OAuth access the official documentation available at `https://twitteroauth.com/`.

The Module directory structure

Initially create the following directories that will be part of the new module:

- `<magento_root>/app/code/Packt/SweetTweet`
- `<magento_root>/app/code/Packt/SweetTweet/Block`
- `<magento_root>/app/code/Packt/SweetTweet/Controller`
- `<magento_root>/app/code/Packt/SweetTweet/Controller/Index`
- `<magento_root>/app/code/Packt/SweetTweet/Controller/Magento2`
- `<magento_root>/app/code/Packt/SweetTweet/Controller/MagentoDev`
- `<magento_root>/app/code/Packt/SweetTweet/Controller/MagentoLive`
- `<magento_root>/app/code/Packt/SweetTweet/etc`
- `<magento_root>/app/code/Packt/SweetTweet/etc/frontend`
- `<magento_root>/app/code/Packt/SweetTweet/Observer`
- `<magento_root>/app/code/Packt/SweetTweet/view`
- `<magento_root>/app/code/Packt/SweetTweet/view/frontend/layout`
- `<magento_root>/app/code/Packt/SweetTweet/view/frontend/templates`
- `<magento_root>/app/code/Packt/SweetTweet/view/frontend/web/css/source`

You don't have to worry at the moment about each directory specification created. They will be detailed in the development sequence.

Coding the composer.json file

Create the `composer.json` file in the root directory of your `SweetTweet` module and insert the following code:

```
{
  "name": "packt/sweet-tweet",
  "description": "Tweet Magento Module - Packt Publishing",
  "type": "magento2-module",
  "version": "1.0.0",
  "license": [
    "OSL-3.0",
    "AFL-3.0"
  ],
  "require": {
    "abraham/twitteroauth": "^0.6.2"
```

```
    },
    "autoload": {
      "files": [ "registration.php" ],
      "psr-4": {
        "Packt\\SweetTweet": ""
      }
    }
  }
```

In the `composer.json` file the names of the module, version, type, as well as the licenses that are applied are declared. Open Software License 3 (`https://opensource.org/license s/OSL-3.0`) and Academic Free License (`https://opensource.org/licenses/AFL-3.0`).

The module dependencies are declared as versions of PHP language by the declaration `"php": "5.5.0|~ 5.6.0|~7.0.0"`. The most important point however in the declaration is the dependence of the package `TwitterOAuth` `"abraham/twitteroauth": "^ 0.6.2"` which is the minimum necessary prerequisite to run the `SweetTweet` module.

In the `autoload` declaration, the `registration.php` file is declared to be loaded accompanied of the convention name `Packt\SweetTweet` linked directly to **PHP Standards Recommendations (PSR) 4 – Autoloader**. In the next chapter, a more detailed way to adopt PSRs on Magento 2 will be approached.

Open the terminal or the prompt command to access the root directory of your `SweetTweet` module and run the following command:

```
composer install --no-autoloader
```

This command will make the Twitter OAuth installation on the `Packt/SweetTweet/vendor` directory. The packages will be included on the `registration.php` in the next sequence.

```
SunnyGo:SweetTweet fjmiguel$ composer install
Loading composer repositories with package information
Updating dependencies (including require-dev)
  - Installing abraham/twitteroauth (0.6.4)
    Downloading: 100%

Writing lock file
Generating autoload files
```

It is important to reiterate that the Composer installs the packages that are available on **Packagist** (`https://packagist.org/`). Once we have the TwitterOAuth available on Packagist, it is possible to automate the management of its dependence on the `SweetTweet` module:

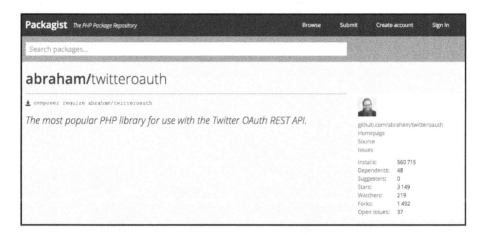

The `vendor` directory will have the following provision:

Declaring the XML configuration files and registration.php

Create the `registration.php` file on the `Packt/SweetTweet/` directory with the following codification:

```php
<?php
\Magento\Framework\Component\ComponentRegistrar::register(
    \Magento\Framework\Component\ComponentRegistrar::MODULE,
    'Packt_SweetTweet',
    __DIR__
);

require_once __DIR__ . "/vendor/abraham/twitteroauth/autoload.php";
```

Besides the instructions that you already know, you will also require the instruction `require_once "/vendor/abraham/twitteroauth/autoload.php"` which will be responsible for loading the package `TwitterOAuth` using the Autoloader (PSR-4) concept. This instruction is important because it allows your module to be fully extensible providing for the installation of third-party libraries in a transparent way and which work in your module using the PSR-4 notation.

Now, the basic module settings will be declared in the XML files.

First, create the `module.xml` file for module declaration in the directory `Packt/SweetTweet/etc` on Magento 2:

```xml
<?xml version="1.0"?>
<config xmlns:xsi="http://www.w3.org/2001/XMLSchema-instance"
xsi:noNamespaceSchemaLocation="urn:magento:framework:
Module/etc/module.xsd">
<module name="Packt_SweetTweet" setup_version="1.0.0"/>
</config>
```

Magento 2 works with the validation scheme called **Uniform Resource Names (URN)** as reference to the XML declarations. The tag `<module>` contains the name of the `Vendor` and the module, being a standard nomenclature: `Vendor_Module`.

In the directory, `Packt/SweetTweet/etc/` **frontend** create the `routes.xml` file with the following code:

```xml
<?xml version="1.0"?>
<config xmlns:xsi="http://www.w3.org/2001/XMLSchema-instance"
xsi:noNamespaceSchemaLocation="urn:magento:framework:
App/etc/routes.xsd">
```

```
<router id="standard">
    <route id="sweettweet" frontName="sweettweet">
        <module name="Packt_SweetTweet" />
    </route>
</router>
</config>
```

The `routes.xml` file is responsible for defining which URL will be accessible to the user and, consequently, which Controller will process the request. In this case the module will be accessible from the URL `http://localhost/Packt/SweetTweet`.

In the directory, `Packt/SweetTweet/etc/frontend` create the `events.xml` file with the following code:

```
<?xml version="1.0"?>
<config xmlns:xsi="http://www.w3.org/2001/XMLSchema-instance"
xsi:noNamespaceSchemaLocation="urn:magento:framework:
Event/etc/events.xsd">
    <event name="page_block_html_topmenu_gethtml_before">
        <observer name="Packt_SweetTweet_observer"
instance="Packt\SweetTweet\Observer\Topmenu" />
    </event>
</config>
```

The `events.xml` is declaring one `Observer` in the module that will be responsible for declaring a new menu item on the front-end Magento 2 directing the user to access the `SweetTweet` module. `Observer` is an event handler that listens to events triggered by the user or system. The `<event>` tag is getting the basic information of the top menu block to handle later in PHP code and the `<observer>` tag is declaring the `Topmenu` observer class.

> For more information about Observers in Magento 2 consult the official documentation available at `http://devdocs.magento.com/guides/v2.0/architecture/archi_perspectives/framework.html`.

Programming the controllers

In the directory `Packt/SweetTweet/Controller/Index` create the `Index.php` file with the following code:

```
<?php

    namespace Packt\SweetTweet\Controller\Index;
```

```
class Index extends \Magento\Framework\App\Action\Action{

    protected $resultPageFactory;

    public function __construct(
        \Magento\Framework\App\Action\Context $context,
        \Magento\Framework\View\Result\PageFactory
$resultPageFactory
    ) {
        $this->resultPageFactory = $resultPageFactory;
        parent::__construct($context);
    }

    public function execute(){
        return $this->resultPageFactory->create();
    }
}
```

Now you will create controllers to manage the three distinct layers according to the hashtag. All the controllers will have the nomenclature of the file as Index.php, but in different directories.

In the directory Packt/SweetTweet/Controller/Magento2 create the Index.php controller with the following code:

```
<?php

namespace Packt\SweetTweet\Controller\Magento2;

class Index extends \Magento\Framework\App\Action\Action{

    protected $resultPageFactory;

    public function __construct(
        \Magento\Framework\App\Action\Context $context,
        \Magento\Framework\View\Result\PageFactory
$resultPageFactory
    ) {
        $this->resultPageFactory = $resultPageFactory;
        parent::__construct($context);
    }

    public function execute()
    {
        return $this->resultPageFactory->create();
    }
}
```

In the directory `Packt/SweetTweet/Controller/MagentoDev` create the `Index.php` controller:

```php
<?php

namespace Packt\SweetTweet\Controller\MagentoDev;

class Index extends \Magento\Framework\App\Action\Action{

    protected $resultPageFactory;

    public function __construct(
        \Magento\Framework\App\Action\Context $context,
        \Magento\Framework\View\Result\PageFactory
$resultPageFactory
    ) {
        $this->resultPageFactory = $resultPageFactory;
        parent::__construct($context);
    }

    public function execute()
    {
        return $this->resultPageFactory->create();
    }
}
```

Finally, in the directory `Packt/SweetTweet/Controller/MagentoLive` create the `Index.php` controller:

```php
<?php

namespace Packt\SweetTweet\Controller\MagentoLive;

class Index extends \Magento\Framework\App\Action\Action{

    protected $resultPageFactory;

    public function __construct(
        \Magento\Framework\App\Action\Context $context,
        \Magento\Framework\View\Result\PageFactory
$resultPageFactory
    ) {
        $this->resultPageFactory = $resultPageFactory;
        parent::__construct($context);
    }

    public function execute()
    {
```

```
                return $this->resultPageFactory->create();
            }
        }
```

These controllers will be responsible for creating the rendering of the module home page and the three pages that will display the results of tweets. The rendering according to the access to the module index page is done by the use of `PageFactory` class and its creation is done by the `execute()` method, extending the functionalities of the `Action` class.

The inheritance of the `Action` class provides the functionality to handle actions triggered by the URL access. When the user accesses the URL: `http://localhost/SweetTweet/` the `routes.xml` the file will redirect to the `Index/Index.php` controller to treat the user request made by the access of the URL.

The **Dependency Injection**`Context $context` and `PageFactory $resultPageFactory` in the `__construct()` method are declaring the initial construct of the `Action` class and declaring the View layer to work with the template file.

For more information about the Dependency Injection access the Magento 2 official documentation at `http://devdocs.magento.com/guides/v2.0/ extension-dev-guide/depend-inj.html`.

Programming the blocks

The blocks will be responsible for the declaration of applied logic and to the View layer of `SweetTweet` module. In the directory `Packt/SweetTweet/Block` create the `Index.php` file with the following code:

```php
<?php

namespace Packt\SweetTweet\Block;

class Index extends \Magento\Framework\View\Element\Template{

    public function getMagento2(){
        return $this->getData('urlMagento2');
    }

    public function getMagentoDev(){
        return $this->getData('urlMagentoDev');
    }

    public function getMagentoLive(){
```

```
            return $this->getData('urlMagentoLive');
        }
    }
```

The `getMagento2()`, `getMagentoDev()` and `getMagentoLive()` methods are responsible for collecting the URLs that will be declared in the XML files to the configuration of the View layer extending the `Template` class for access to the `getData()` method.

You will now encode the heart of the Sweet Tweet module. This degree of importance is because of the fact that the block loads the Business layer that effectively give life to the module. To create the `Tweets.php` file in the `Packt/SweetTweet/Block` directory use the following code:

```php
<?php
    namespace Packt\SweetTweet\Block;

    use Abraham\TwitterOAuth\TwitterOAuth;

    class Tweets extends \Magento\Framework\View\Element\Template{

        private $consumerKey;
        private $consumerSecret;
        private $accessToken;
        private $accessTokenSecret;

    public function searchTweets(){
        $connection = $this->twitterDevAuth();
        $result = $connection->get("search/tweets",
array("q" =>$this->getData('hashtag'), "result_type"=>"recent", "count" =>
10));

        return $result->statuses;
    }

    private function twitterDevAuth(){
        $this->consumerKey = YOUR_CONSUMER_KEY;
        $this->consumerSecret = YOUR_CONSUMER_SECRET;
        $this->accessToken = YOUR_ACCESS_TOKEN;
        $this->accessTokenSecret  = YOUR_ACCESS_TOKEN_SECRET;

        return new TwitterOAuth($this->consumerKey, $this->consumerSecret,
$this->accessToken, $this->accessTokenSecret);
    }
    }
```

This block effectively uses the `TwitterOAuth` package that is being declared by the PSR notation `Abraham\TwitterOAuth\TwitterOAuth`. Only here there are two PSR standards used: **PSR-0** and **PSR-4**.

The `searchTweets()` method is responsible for performing the research of the top ten most recent tweets according to #hashtags that will be declared following the sequence on the project layout configuration files.

The `twitterDevAuth()` method authenticates the REST API Twitter.

Programming the Observer

Previously you declared the XML file responsible for the initial indication of the `Observer` that will be responsible for the module inclusion on the top menu. Now, in the directory `Packt/SweetTweet/Observer`, create the `Topmenu.php` observer with the following code:

```php
<?php
namespace Packt\SweetTweet\Observer;

use Magento\Framework\Event\Observer as EventObserver;
use Magento\Framework\Data\Tree\Node;
use Magento\Framework\Event\ObserverInterface;

class Topmenu implements ObserverInterface{

    /**
     * @param EventObserver $observer
     * @return $this
     */
    public function execute(EventObserver $observer)
    {

    $urlInterface = \Magento\Framework\App\
ObjectManager::getInstance()->
get('Magento\Framework\UrlInterface');

    $active = strpos($urlInterface->getCurrentUrl(), "sweettweet");

      $menu = $observer->getMenu();
      $tree = $menu->getTree();
      $data = [
          'name'   => __("SweetTweet"),
          'id'     => 'tweetsmenu',
          'url'    => $urlInterface->getBaseUrl() . 'sweettweet',
          'is_active' => $active
```

```
        ];
        $node = new Node($data, 'id', $tree, $menu);
        $menu->addChild($node);
        return $this;
    }
}
```

The `Topmenu.php` dynamically creates a new item for the Sweet Tweet module by adding a node in the top menu link schema. The `ObjectManager::getInstance()->get('Magento\Framework\UrlInterface')` gets the base URL and the current URL to create the specific link to Sweet Tweet module. The `observer` works dynamically with the **Document Object Model** (**DOM**) concept of node and trees.

Programming the View layer

You have already prepared all the logical functioning scheme of the Sweet Tweet module, and it is now necessary to create rules of View templates and effectively provide access to the user.

 Remember that the default configuration of layout declarations that take care of template files is `<module_name>_<controller>_<controller_file>.xml`.

Now, working with the `Packt/SweetTweet/view/frontend/layout` directory declare the `sweettweet_index_index.xml` file as follows:

```xml
<?xml version="1.0"?>
<page xmlns:xsi="http://www.w3.org/2001/XMLSchema-instance"
layout="1column"
xsi:noNamespaceSchemaLocation="urn:magento:framework:View/Layout/etc/page_c
onfiguration.xsd">
    <head>
        <title>
            SweetTweet PacktModule
        </title>
    </head>
    <body>
        <referenceContainer name="content">
            <block class="Packt\SweetTweet\Block\Index"
 template="Packt_SweetTweet::index.phtml">
                <arguments>
                    <argument name="urlMagento2"
```

```
xsi:type="url" path="sweettweet/magento2" />
                    <argument name="urlMagentoLive"
xsi:type="url" path="sweettweet/magentolive" />
                    <argument name="urlMagentoDev"
xsi:type="url" path="sweettweet/magentodev" />
                </arguments>
            </block>
        </referenceContainer>
    </body>
</page>
```

The `<block>` tag is binding the block `Index.php` to the `index.phtml` template. The `<arguments>` tag is transporting three URL parameters to the block. These parameters will be used in `index.phtml` file.

In the same directory, you will declare three more configuration files that will be responsible for taking care of the templates that display the tweets according to the hashtag.

Declare the `sweettweet_magento2_index.xml` file:

```
<?xml version="1.0"?>
<page xmlns:xsi="http://www.w3.org/2001/XMLSchema-instance"
layout="1column" xsi:noNamespaceSchemaLocation="urn:magento:framework:
View/Layout/etc/page_configuration.xsd">
    <head>
        <title>
            SweetTweet #Magento2
        </title>
        <css src="Packt_SweetTweet::css/source/module.css"/>
    </head>
    <body>
        <referenceContainer name="content">
            <block class="Packt\SweetTweet\Block\Tweets"
template="Packt_SweetTweet::tweets.phtml">
                <arguments>
                    <argument name="hashtag"xsi:type="string">
#magento2
</argument>
                </arguments>
            </block>
        </referenceContainer>
    </body>
</page>
```

Declare the file `sweettweet_magentodev_index.xml`:

```
<?xml version="1.0"?>
<page xmlns:xsi="http://www.w3.org/2001/XMLSchema-instance"
```

```xml
layout="1column" xsi:noNamespaceSchemaLocation="urn:magento:framework:
View/Layout/etc/page_configuration.xsd">
    <head>
        <title>
            SweetTweet #MagentoDev
        </title>
        <css src="Packt_SweetTweet::css/source/module.css"/>
    </head>
    <body>
        <referenceContainer name="content">
            <block class="Packt\SweetTweet\Block\Tweets"
template="Packt_SweetTweet::tweets.phtml">
                <arguments>
                    <argument name="hashtag" xsi:type="string">
#magentodev
</argument>
                </arguments>
            </block>
        </referenceContainer>
    </body>
</page>
```

Declare the file sweettweet_magentolive_index.xml:

```xml
<?xml version="1.0"?>
<page xmlns:xsi="http://www.w3.org/2001/XMLSchema-instance"
layout="1column" xsi:noNamespaceSchemaLocation="urn:magento:framework:
View/Layout/etc/page_configuration.xsd">
    <head>
        <title>
            SweetTweet #MagentoLive
        </title>
        <css src="Packt_SweetTweet::css/source/module.css"/>
    </head>
    <body>
        <referenceContainer name="content">
            <block class="Packt\SweetTweet\Block\Tweets"
template="Packt_SweetTweet::tweets.phtml">
                <arguments>
                    <argument name="hashtag" xsi:type="string">
#magentolive
</argument>
                </arguments>
            </block>
        </referenceContainer>
    </body>
</page>
```

The `<css>` element is responsible for loading the module `css`. The `<block>` tag is binding the block `Tweets.php` to the `tweets.phtml` template. The `<argument name="hashtag">` is transporting the hashtag parameter to the `Tweets.php` block to search the last mentions of the specific hashtag in the Twitter database.

Once the settings of the templates are ready, it is time to code the template files. In the directory `Packt/SweetTweet/view/frontend/templates` you will encode two distinct templates. The first will be the module index page and the second will have the purpose of displaying the tweet results according to the #hashtag selected.

Create the `index.phtml` file with the following code:

```
<h2><?php echo __('Recent Tweets:')?></h2>
<ul>
  <li>
    <a href="<?php echo $block->escapeHtml($block->getMagento2()) ?>">
      <span><?php echo __('Magento2')?></span>
    </a>
  </li>
  <li>
    <a href="<?php echo $block->escapeHtml($block->getMagentoDev()) ?>">
      <span><?php echo __('MagentoDev')?></span>
    </a>
  </li>
  <li>
    <a href="<?php echo $block->escapeHtml($block->getMagentoLive()) ?>">
      <span><?php echo __('MagentoLive')?></span>
    </a>
  </li>
</ul>
```

The `$block` object has access to the methods of `Block/Index.php` and the URL of the pages are building dynamically.

Now create the file `tweets.phtml`:

```
<?php
  $tweets = $block->searchTweets();
?>

<div id="wrapper">
  <div id="columns">
    <?php foreach ($tweets as $tweet){ ?>
        <div class="tweet">
         <p>
           <a href="https://twitter.com/intent/user?user_id=
<?php echo $tweet->user->id; ?>" target="_blank">
```

```
                    <img src="<?php
echo $tweet->user->profile_image_url; ?>"
            alt="profile">
                    <?php echo $tweet->user->name; ?>
                </a>
            <br />
<?php echo __('Created:')?> <?php echo $tweet->created_at; ?>
            <br /><br />
<a href="<?php echo isset($tweet->entities->urls[0]->url) ?
            $tweet->entities->urls[0]->url : "#"; ?>"
target="_blank"><?php echo $tweet->text;?></a>
<?php echo $tweet->text;?>

            </a>
        </p>
    </div>
    <?php } ?>
    </div>
</div>
</div>
```

The `searchTweets()` method is iterating over the results obtained by accessing the JSON response sent by the REST API Twitter and writing the URL to access the tweet by `$tweet->statement->entities->urls[0]->url`, as well as displaying user information, creation date, and tweet.

To finish the View layer, declare the file `module.less` in the directory `Packt/SweetTweet/view/frontend/web/css/source`, which will be the CSS / LESS stylesheet:

```
@media (min-width: 960px){
#wrapper {
width: 90%;
max-width: 1100px;
min-width: 800px;
margin: 50px auto;
}

    #columns {
    -webkit-column-count: 3;
  -webkit-column-gap: 10px;
    -webkit-column-fill: auto;
  -moz-column-count: 3;
    -moz-column-gap: 10px;
  -moz-column-fill: auto;
    column-count: 3;
  column-gap: 15px;
    column-fill: auto;
```

```
      }
  }

.tweet {
  display: inline-block;
  background: #FEFEFE;
  border: 2px solid #FAFAFA;
  box-shadow: 0 1px 2px rgba(34, 25, 25, 0.4);
  margin: 0 2px 15px;
  -webkit-column-break-inside: avoid;
  -moz-column-break-inside: avoid;
  column-break-inside: avoid;
  padding: 15px;
  padding-bottom: 5px;
  background: -webkit-linear-gradient(45deg, #FFF, #F9F9F9);
  opacity: 1;

  -webkit-transition: all .2s ease;
  -moz-transition: all .2s ease;
  -o-transition: all .2s ease;
  transition: all .2s ease;
}

.tweet img {
  width: 15%;
  display:block;
  float:left;
  margin: 0px 5px 0px 0px;
}

.tweet p {
  font: 12px/18px Arial, sans-serif;
  color: #333;
  margin: 0;
}

#columns:hover .img:not(:hover) {
  opacity: 0.4;
}
```

Done! After too much work it is time to activate the module in Magento 2.

Enabling the module

At the end you basically have the following `SweetTweet` module directory structure:

Notice that you worked on all layers of the Magento 2 system components to create a unique solution for your instance. Too much work here, isn't it? But it was definitely worth it.

Now it's time to have your efforts rewarded by activating the module. Follow the step by step instructions to active the module in your Magento 2 instance:

- Access the terminal or the command prompt of your root directory of Magento 2
- Run the command `php bin/magento module:enable --clear-static-content Packt_SweetTweet`
- * Run the command `php bin/magento setup:upgrade`

Take a look at the following screenshot:

```
SunnyGo:magento2 fjmiguel$ php bin/magento module:enable --clear-static-content Packt_SweetTweet
The following modules have been enabled:
[- Packt_SweetTweet

To make sure that the enabled modules are properly registered, run 'setup:upgrade'.
Cache cleared successfully.
Generated classes cleared successfully. Please re-run Magento compile command
Generated static view files cleared successfully.
```

With the activated module, it is necessary to run the Grunt scripts and make a new deployment of static files in your Magento 2 instance:

- Run the commands `grunt clean:bookstore_en_US` and `grunt clean:bookstore_de_DE`
- Run the commands `grunt exec:bookstore_en_US` and `grunt exec:bookstore_de_DE`
- Run the commands `grunt less:bookstore_en_US` and `grunt less:bookstore_de_DE`
- Run the command `php bin/magento setup:static-content:deploy en_US de_DE`
- Lastly, run the command `php bin/magento cache:clean`

Access your Magento 2 local instance and check that you now have an item of a new menu called `SweetTweet` with the following content:

This home page contains links that will direct you to the Tweets pages. Click on any of the links to view how the Tweets will be displayed:

Summary

In this chapter, you practiced more concepts about Magento Theme development. Specifically, you developed a new module using the techniques learned in the previous chapters and adding more new techniques to improve your knowledge in developing Magento 2 themes.

You practiced the creation of templates, configuration files, URL routing besides the integration of distinct components of Magento 2.

Despite the book's focus on theme development, I will reiterate one more time the importance of having knowledge about the interaction among the components in order to create customized solutions and more options for users, companies, and clients.

Keep going on investigating techniques and solutions for improvement. All of these techniques can be improved! Like all software, it is always evolving.

In the next chapter, you will see best practices for Magento 2 theme development. See you then.

11

Theme Development Best Practices

"Don't only practice your art, but force your way into its secrets; art deserves that, for it and knowledge can raise man to the Divine."
– Ludwig van Beethoven

In this chapter, we will delve deeper into Magento 2 module development. This is a big professional differential that you can create Magento 2 increasingly customized solutions. The importance of knowing the different layers and the interactions among the distinct components of Magento 2 increasingly contributes to your improvement and especially to the quality you will deliver in your projects.

In the previous chapter, you used the jCarousel library to enrich your theme project. In this chapter, you will make a direct integration with the Twitter REST API.

The following topics will be covered:

- Magento components
- Development workflow
- Developing the Sweet Tweet module

Why I should worry about it?

With the present advent of agile software development, we're increasingly seeing that developers who create a conducive environment for incremental improvements in their code deliver great value in the shortest possible time. To achieve this kind of maturity, it is necessary that professionals follow the evolution of technology, perform tests, and incorporate innovations that increase productivity in their projects and tools.

Studying the techniques that bring this benefit is very important so that we can achieve significant results as professionals in the technology area.

Until now, you realize that Magento 2 the solutions-development universe is wide and its architecture provides space for modular growth not only of themes, which are the main focus of the book, but also to modules and distinct languages that you want to use in your solutions.

For this organization to be possible between all the functional components, it is important that your code behaves according to the Magento 2 system architecture.

In a survey shown in the Magento developers area (`http://devdocs.magento.com/guides /v2.0/ext-best-practices/bk-ext-best-practices.html`), the distribution of used instances versus the quantity of extensions is as follows:

Edition	1-9 extensions	10-30 extensions	31-50 extensions	50+ extensions
Community	10%	53%	26%	11%
Enterprise	9%	32%	27%	32%

Note that the Community Edition and Enterprise Edition should work with more than ten extensions or modules simultaneously, so that the system runs in a transparent way and in accordance with the expectations of your users.

The evolution of Magento from version 1 to version 2 made these concepts even more evident once a series of standards had been adopted to aim for delivery quality and componentization of its modules, aiming to extend its functionality. How about a little more understanding of these standards?

Best practices in Magento 2 development

In the previous chapters, the concern about layout configuration files and theme declaration was evident in the theme development process, making it necessary for us to follow specific standards for proper functioning in the instance. Besides the correct declaration, it is necessary that the codification follow standards of quality and functionality within the proposed architecture.

Magento 2 uses the standards provided by **Zend Coding Standards** and by the **PHP Framework Interop Group**, which decide the format in which themes and modules must operate in the Magento system.

 For more information about the Zend Coding Standards, refer to the official documentation at `https://framework.zend.com/manual/1.12/en/coding-standard.html`.

The developed code should make the most of the existing code in the Magento 2 system. For example, during the development of the Bookstore theme, we used all of the initial structure of the Blank theme in addition to the Luma theme with the instruction `<parent>Magento/luma</parent>` in the `theme.xml` file, so you could focus only on customizations to be applied. Still, as an example, in the Promo module, you used the Model/Class `CategoryFactory` and the `getProductCollection()` method to list the products in jCarousel.

The code-writing process should focus only on your most important deliverable (defined goal), taking advantage of a system that already provides a complete solution. All your code must be testable in small pieces and validated incrementally so that you avoid unnecessary bugs.

It is interesting that we have a dedicated area for testability in Magento 2:

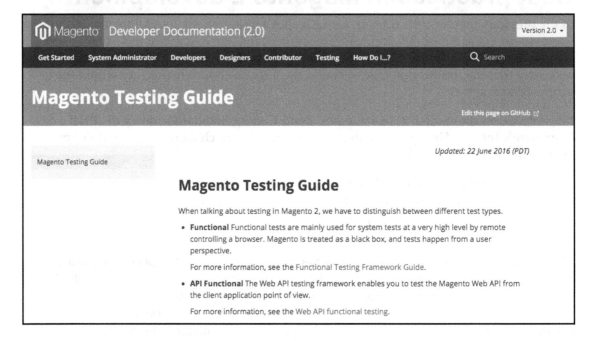

Although it is not in the scope of this book, it is totally advisable that you research more about the testing area. It has gained a lot of strength just due to the growth of agile software development and, specifically, on Magento 2 for validation and quality compared to the standards established as best practices.

Specifically, in the development of Magento 2 themes, a lot of attention was paid to RWD in developed projects because the whole developed view layer works well on many devices, which requires a responsive approach in order to show the content without the user facing any loss in quality:

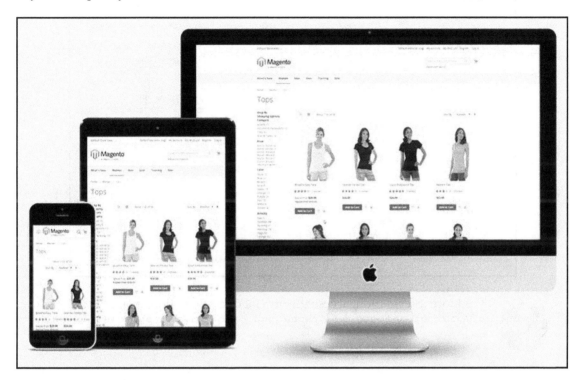

Another good recommendation that can be used in Magento theme development is the maintenance of the **Magento 2 cache system**. It can happen that, during development, you notice differences between the code you just edited and the final result shown in the browser. This error is more common than you might think. The adoption of Grunt.js is a great help in the development process because it automates the process, generating greater dynamics in the development of your themes. Anyway, you can manage the cache system from the administrative panel or using the **Magento CLI** tool, cleaning and even disabling the cache if necessary.

During development, it is necessary that you maintain the following directories that generate temporary information about the Magento 2 system:

Directory	What it contains
var/page_cache	Cached pages from the full page cache mechanism. (This directory is empty if you use a third-party HTTP accelerator like Varnish.)
var/cache	All cacheable objects *except* the page cache. (This directory is empty if you use a third-party cache storage like Redis.)
var/composer_home	Home directory for the Setup Wizard artifacts. Typically, you shouldn't touch this directory; clear it only if you're an experienced developer and are familiar with the Magento plug-in.
	For example, if the Component Manager or System Upgrade web-based utilities cannot find the correct components you can try clearing this directory; however, doing so adversely affects the performance of those utilities.
var/generation	Contains generated code.
var/di	Contains the compiled dependency injection configuration for all modules.
var/view_preprocessed	Minified templates and compiled LESS (meaning LESS, CSS, and HTML).

For more information, access the official documentation, available at `http ://devdocs.magento.com/guides/v2.0/howdoi/php/php_clear-dirs.h tml`.

Always use the Magento architecture

As seen in `Chapter 3`, *Magento 2 Theme Layout*, the Magento system uses MVC concepts. This standard provides the segmentation of different system components, aiming at better use of its resources and providing modularity in developing solutions and customizing architecture.

For all development that is performed in the system, it is strongly recommended you use the architecture aiming for standard maintenance to share your solutions between different instances and projects.

During the development of the Bookstore theme, we used the
`app/design/frontend/Packt/bookstore` directory, inheriting the Blank and Luma
theme features but not changing them directly. For the development of the modules, we
used the `app/code/Packt` directory but without directly changing the modules that
supported the development of the new module, such as the product catalog module used to
power the operation of jCarousel.

These techniques reinforce another good practice: you should not change the core of the
Magento 2 system. In order to not jeopardize the updates that occur periodically and
provide better distribution of your customizations between different Magento 2 instances, it
is recommended that you use techniques such as overrides and observers, among others
learned in this book.

The current Magento 2 system architecture is arranged as follows:

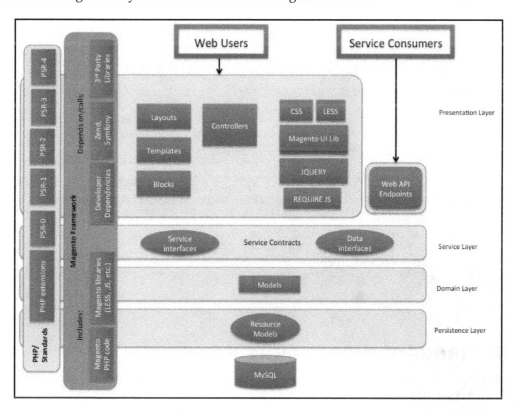

For more information about the use of the Magento 2 architecture, refer to the official documentation at `http://devdocs.magento.com/guides/v2.0/ext-best-practices/extension-coding/working-with-arch-bp.html`.

The Magento technology stack

The Magento 2 stack is well diversified. This is why it is strongly recommended that you at least know the position of each element and the contribution it makes to the Magento system as a whole.

Keeping this book's scope in mind, I'll quote the following stack and sources of research:

- HTML5: `https://www.w3.org/TR/html5/`
- CSS3: `https://www.w3.org/TR/CSS/`
- jQuery: `http://jquery.com/`
- RequireJS: `http://requirejs.org/`
- Knockout.js: `http://knockoutjs.com/`
- Zend Framework: `https://framework.zend.com/`
- Symfony: `https://symfony.com/`
- Coding standards PSR: `http://www.php-fig.org/`

The sources have been quoted here for you to interact with these elements and explore their functionalities inside the Magento 2 architecture in order to learn the best techniques to be employed in your future Magento projects.

 If you want to find out more about the stack that is part of the Magento 2 system, access the official documentation available at `http://devdocs.magento.com/guides/v2.0/architecture/tech-stack.html`.

PHP standard recommendations

The Magento 2 system uses recommended standards of PHP coding developed by **The PHP Framework Interop Group** (`http://www.php-fig.org`), which aims to create standardization and high-level collaboration for PHP development.

In addition to recommendations that are in the draft or accepted stages, there are currently 17 different standards for PHP coding standardization being debated on the website.

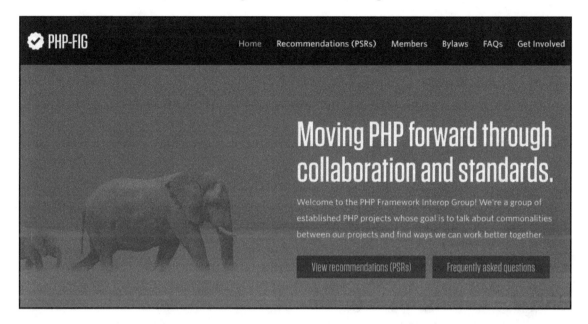

The importance of knowing these patterns and understanding their context in the Magento 2 system can be the difference between developing themes with low and high quality.

We will now look at the main patterns used in the Magento 2 system.

PSR-1 – basic coding standards

To standardize code according to established standards, it is recommended you adhere to the following during Magento 2 code development:

- PHP code can only begin with the `<?php` and `<?=` tags
- Namespaces and classes must follow the autoloading technique-`PSR`: `[PSR-0, PSR-4]`
- Class names must be declared in the `MyClass` format:

```php
<?php
namespace Vendor\Model;
class MyClass
{
}
```

- Class constants must be declared all in upper case with underscore separators:

```php
<?php
namespace Vendor\Model;
class MyClass
{
const MAGENTO_VERSION = '2.1';
}
```

- Method names must be declared in the `myMethod()` format:

```php
<?php
namespace Vendor\Model;
class MyClass
{
const MAGENTO_VERSION = '2.1';
    myMethod()
    {
    }
}
```

PSR-2 – coding style guide

The main objective of the PSR-2 standard is to create standards so that developed code is easily understood by the many developers who will work on the same code. Now imagine if this standard had not been adopted by the Magento 2 system. With an active community, it could hardly exponentially grow the project, as has been happening over the years of its existence.

The styles and code patterns can be classified as follows:

- The code must follow the `PSR [PSR-1]` pattern, being an extension of the same
- In your code, you must use four spaces instead of a Tab character
- Limit each line to 80 characters
- There must be a blank line after the namespace declaration
- The open key for classes and methods must be declared on the next line, and its closure must be in the second-last line of the code
- An opening parenthesis for control structures must not have a space after your declaration or its closing parenthesis after your closure
- Look at the following example code to understand better:

```php
<?php
namespace Vendor\Package;
```

```
use FooInterface;
use BarClass as Bar;
use OtherVendor\OtherPackage\BazClass;
class Foo extends Bar implements FooInterface
{
    public function sampleFunction($a, $b = null)
    {
        if ($a === $b) {
            bar();
        } elseif ($a > $b) {
            $foo->bar($arg1);
        } else {
            BazClass::bar($arg2, $arg3);
        }
    }

    final public static function bar()
    {
        // method body
    }
}
```

PSR-4 – autoloader

The **PSR-4** standard is widely used in the Magento 2 system. Its main objective is to load classes in a standardized way and automate the classes to be used in the code that you are developing.

PSR-4 is similar to the PSR-0 standard; however, the standard in question is deprecated and PSR-4 is used by convention instead.

The following characteristics are part of the PSR-4 standard:

- The use of best practices for class-declaration autoloaders is also known as fully qualified class name
- The term `class` refers to classes, interfaces, traits, and other similar structures
- It is recommend that you use the following format for declaring namespaces:
  `\<NameSpaceName>(\<SubNamespaceNames>)*\<ClassName>`
- All namespace names must start with `Vendor` in order to distribute functionality
- In the namespace declaration, you should have the class name to be used in your code at the end of the declaration
- Underscores have no special meaning in any portion of the class name

- Alphabetic characters can be a combination of lowercase and uppercase
- All class names are case sensitive

For more information about PSR-4, refer to the official documentation, available at `http://www.php-fig.org/psr/psr-4/`.

Strategies for customizing your themes

All good professionals must draw clear and concise strategies for the development of their solutions. With the techniques we've seen, you will already be able to develop your themes; however, it is important to have some things cleared before you code your solution.

Despite the knowledge, you must have in relation to the Magento 2 structure with respect to both the coding architecture and use of the PHP language as the best practice for codification, the layer that you will be acting, with greater emphasis is the system's presentation layer. In this layer, you will be developing interactions and interfaces using HTML 5, CSS 3, and PHTML files for the effective presentation of all content with a few snippets of PHP code. For the presentation layer, the focus will be on theme development, which is also the focus of this book.

First of all, you must study the area that you intend to develop your theme in (pet shop, games shop, clothing store, and so on), looking for ideas and solutions already existing in the market in order to bring greater value to your client and/or project. Always keep in mind that you use the `Vendor/Theme` directory structure to deploy your themes so that you can better separate your project, creating more than one theme for a specific `Vendor` directory.

After this step, it is important to define which technologies are available in addition to the Magento 2 architecture (third-party libraries) that you will use in your project so that you can define the best strategy for using the resources already available.

Magento 2 visualization elements are very important in this process. The Magento UI library and Magento components contain a substantial suite, so you can use more resources in your projects. With the technique of using blocks and containers, you will be able to define the behavior of your new theme in many different presentation layers. Recall that both blocks as containers act as follows:

- Blocks generate dynamic content
- Containers collect an ordered group of child view elements

Always keep in mind the content delivery flow to which the Magento 2 system adheres, according to its architecture: the users interact with the components of the presentation layer, which generates calls to services, modules, business rules, and the presentation page according to the navigation performed. Each user action calls the service of a specific module within the architecture. For example, browsing the category page of a particular product fires presentation processes PHTML files contained in the product catalog module and often involves interacting with custom CSS/LESS and PHTML files developed for the theme.

Use the preexisting components to your advantage to assist you in developing customized solutions for the Magento 2 system. The customization implemented in the Magento system can be divided into four distinct types, as follows:

- **Extend Magento-provided CSS**: It is possible, using only CSS, to customize themes by applying a new visual concept to your project. This type of technique is used for projects that do not require a large budget as well as projects that need to be published in a short time.
- **Replace PHTML template files**: Instead of creating a new style sheet, you can change the nature of the HTML code contained in your PHTML files. This option also allows you to incorporate or edit snippets in PHP and JavaScript.
- **Replace Magento-provided CSS**: Use a new design style sheet in your Magento theme, aiming at delivering a new layout experience to your customer and Magento 2 project.
- **Replace Magento-provided CSS, HTML, and JavaScript**: Develop a totally new project by changing the default schema and initial structure that Magento 2 provides for its development community. This step is now necessary to create a high degree of maturity in the Magento architecture so that development is done according to good practice and established standards.

Seeking external resources to improve

Seek external resources that can enrich your knowledge of the stack used for the development of Magento 2; this will prove very important since the design of the final Magento product is a culmination of best practices and techniques developed by several professionals in their respective areas.

Among the resources available are discussion forums, official documentation, a community of developers, books, blogs, and free courses such as **Coursera** (http://www.coursera.or g), **Udemy** (https://www.udemy.com), and **edX** (https://www.edx.org).

 In free courses websites, you will find a lot of study material on backend and frontend web development as well as programming techniques.

I will now highlight some of the resources focused on Magento that you can help you in your research and studies.

Community Magento

The **Magento forums** (https://community.magento.com/) are forums where you can connect with other professionals and debate issues relating to technologies, extensions, themes, and functionalities of versions 1 and 2 of Magento.

The developer community is very active and can help you in your projects and learning, based on problems reported by members. Participate and collaborate.

The Magento 2 official repository

You can collaborate and follow the evolution the Magento 2 system according to the pull request, issues, and commits that are made by the Magento 2 developer community.

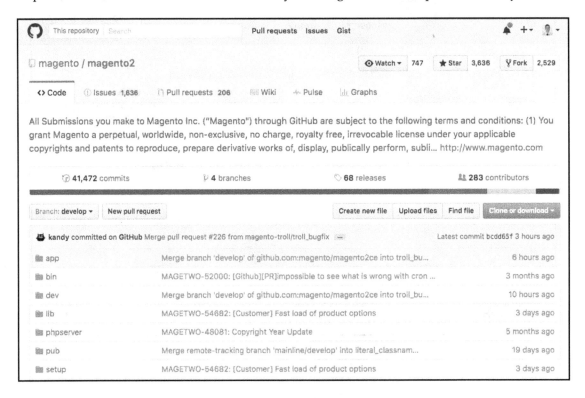

In case you do not have much experience with GitHub, it is strongly recommended that you start to learn about the way to work in teams using software versioning. For more information about Git, I suggest reading the Pro Git book, available at `https://git-scm.co m/book/en/v2`.

The Magento blog

The official Magento blog (`https://magento.com/blog/tag/magento-2`) is a place where you can follow hot news about the e-commerce market and especially the Magento platform, its innovations, and trends in the adoption of new technologies and techniques.

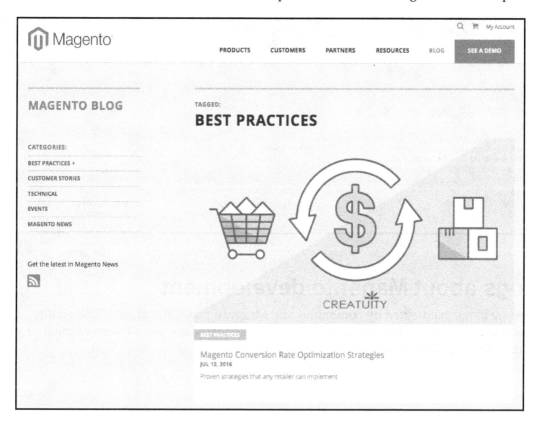

Magento Stack Exchange

Magento Stack Exchange (`http://magento.stackexchange.com/`) is a dedicated forum for Magento developers, focused on questions and answers about development in Magento 2. You can participate in, contribute to, and seek help from the development community.

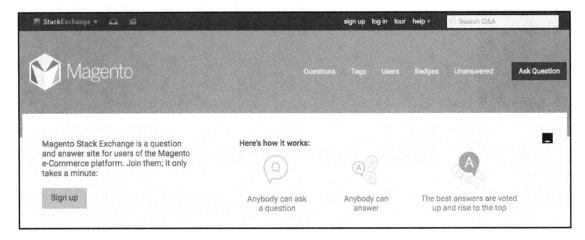

Blogs about Magento development

There are blogs maintained by companies and Magento professionals that add quality content to the Magento development community. I'll introduce you to some of them so you can read some quality content and improve your skills.

Inchoo

Inchoo (`http://inchoo.net/`) is a Magento company founded in 2008 in Osijek, Croatia, with a strong focus on providing solutions for e-commerce businesses. Besides having experience in the field, they keep a very good blog (`http://inchoo.net/category/magent o-2/`) full of information for Magento 2 developers.

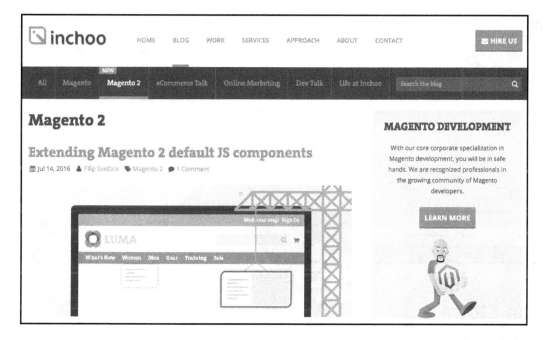

Mukesh Chapagain

The Mukesh Chapagain developer's blog (`http://blog.chapagain.com.np/`) contains excellent material about Magento techniques and is updated regularly.

Alan Storm

The Alan Storm blog is a blog for Magento professionals by Alan Storm (`http://alanstorm.com/`). For many years, it has produced quality material for Magento. You can follow techniques, technologies, and best practices used in Magento 2 development.

Alan Storm
the professional weblog; because we have to;

Home Archive Projects Contact

● **Article Categories**

Magento
Magento 2
Laravel
OroCRM
Modern PHP
SugarCRM
Drupal
WebOS (HP/Palm)
Python
AppleScript
Links (beta)

Magento 2 Articles for Professional Programmers

A growing list of articles plumbing the depths of the enigmatic, and increasingly dominant, Magento eCommerce System, version 2.0.

> Like these articles? Then you'll love Commerce Bug, the must have debugging extension for anyone using Magento. Whether you're just starting out or you're a seasoned pro, Commerce Bug will save you and your team hours everyday. Grab a copy and start working **with** Magento instead of against it.

Magento 2 for PHP MVC Developers
Everything a PHP developer coming to Magento 2 needs to know.

1. Introduction to Magento 2 — No More MVC

2. Magento 2: Serving Frontend Files

3. Magento 2: Adding Frontend Files to your Module

4. Magento 2: Code Generation with Pestle

5. Magento 2: Adding Javascript and CSS via Layout XML

Summary

In this chapter, you learned about the best practices, standards, and sources of research and study for improving your Magento 2 theme development techniques. In the last chapter of the book, you will learn techniques for distributing your themes on Magento Connect.

12
Magento Theme Distribution

"Invention is not enough. Tesla invented the electric power we use, but he struggled to get it out to people. You have to combine both things: invention and innovation focus, plus the company that can commercialize things and get them to people"
– Larry Page

In this final chapter of the book, you will learn the process of sharing, code hosting, validating, and publishing your subject as well as future components (extensions/modules) that you develop for Magento 2.

The following topics will be covered:

- The packaging process
- Packaging your theme
- Hosting your theme
- The Magento marketplace

The packaging process

For every theme you develop for distribution in marketplaces and repositories through the sale and delivery of projects to clients and contractors of the service, you must follow some mandatory requirements for the theme to be packaged properly and consequently distributed to different Magento instances.

As seen in previous chapters, Magento uses the `composer.json` file to define dependencies and information relevant to the developed component. Remember how the `composer.json` file is declared in the Bookstore theme:

```
{
    "name": "packt/bookstore",
    "description": "BookStore theme",
    "require": {
        "php": "~5.5.0|~5.6.0|~7.0.0",
        "magento/theme-frontend-luma": "~100.0",
        "magento/framework": "~100.0"
    },
    "type": "magento2-theme",
    "version": "1.0.0",
    "license": [
        "OSL-3.0",
        "AFL-3.0"
    ],
    "autoload": {
        "files": [ "registration.php" ],
        "psr-4": {
          "Packt\\BookStore": ""
        }
    }
}
```

The main fields of the declaration components in the `composer.json` file are as follows:

- **Name**: A fully qualified component name
- **Type**: This declares the component type
- **Autoload**: This specifies the information necessary to be loaded in the component

The three main types of Magento 2 component declarations can be described as follows:

- **Module**: Use the `magento2-module` type to declare modules that add to and/or modify functionalities in the Magento 2 system
- **Theme**: Use the `magento2-theme` type to declare themes in Magento 2 storefronts
- **Language package**: Use the `magento2-language` type to declare translations in the Magento 2 system

Besides the `composer.json` file that must be declared in the root directory of your theme, you should follow these steps to meet the minimum requirements for packaging your new theme:

1. Register the theme by declaring the `registration.php` file.
2. Package the theme, following the standards set by Magento.
3. Validate the theme before distribution.
4. Publish the theme.

From the minimum requirements mentioned, you already are familiar with the `composer.json` and `registration.php` files. Now we will look at the packaging process, validation, and publication in sequence.

Packaging your theme

By default, all themes should be compressed in ZIP format and contain only the root directory of the component developed, excluding any file and directory that is not part of the standard structure.

The following command shows the compression standard used in Magento 2 components:

```
zip -r vendor-name_package-name-1.0.0.zip package-path/* -x 'package-
path/.git/*'
```

Here, the name of the ZIP file has the following components:

- **vendor**: This symbolizes the vendor by which the theme was developed
- **name_package**: This is the package name
- **name**: This is the component name
- **1.0.0**: This is the component version

After formatting the component name, it defines which directory will be compressed, followed by the `-x` parameter, which excludes the `git` directory from the theme compression.

How about applying ZIP compression on the Bookstore theme? To do this, follow these steps:

1. Using a terminal or Command Prompt, access the theme's root directory: `<magento_root>/app/design/frontend/Packt/bookstore`.
2. Run the `zip packt-bookstore-bookstore.1.0.0.zip*-x'.git/*'` command.

Upon successfully executing this command, you will have packed your theme, and your directory will be as follows:

```
[SunnyGo:bookstore fjmiguel$ zip packt-bookstore-bookstore.1.0.0.zip * -x '.git/*'
  adding: Magento_Catalog/ (stored 0%)
  adding: Magento_Theme/ (stored 0%)
  adding: composer.json (deflated 48%)
  adding: etc/ (stored 0%)
  adding: i18n/ (stored 0%)
  adding: media/ (stored 0%)
  adding: registration.php (deflated 38%)
  adding: theme.xml (deflated 33%)
  adding: web/ (stored 0%)
[SunnyGo:bookstore fjmiguel$ ls
Magento_Catalog              i18n                              theme.xml
Magento_Theme                media                             web
composer.json                packt-bookstore-bookstore.1.0.0.zip
etc                          registration.php
SunnyGo:bookstore fjmiguel$ 
```

After this, you will validate your new Magento theme using a verification tool.

Magento component validation

The Magento developer community created the `validate_m2_package` script to perform validation of components developed for Magento 2. This script is available on the GitHub repository of the Magento 2 development community in the `marketplace-tools` directory:

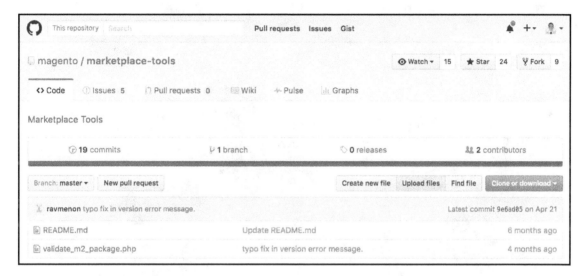

According to the description, the idea behind **Marketplace Tools** is to house standalone tools that developers can use to validate and verify their extensions before submitting them to the Marketplace.

Here's how to use the validation tool:

1. Download the `validate_m2_package.php` script, available at `https://github .com/magento/marketplace-tools`.
2. Move the script to the root directory of the Bookstore theme `<magento_root>/app/design/frontend/Packt/bookstore`.
3. Open a terminal or Command Prompt.
4. Run the `validate_m2_package.php packt-bookstore-bookstore.1.0.0.zip` PHP command.

This command will validate the package you previously created with the ZIP command. If all goes well, you will not have any response from the command line, which will mean that your package is in line with the minimum requirements for publication.

If you wish, you can use the -d parameter that enables you to debug your component by printing messages during verification. To use this option, run the following command:

```
php validate_m2_package.php -d packt-bookstore-bookstore.1.0.0.zip
```

If everything goes as expected, the response will be as follows:

```
[SunnyGo:bookstore fjmiguel$ php validate_m2_package.php -d packt-bookstore-bookstore.1.0.0.zip
DEBUG - "packt-bookstore-bookstore.1.0.0.zip": Zip file contents (file and size).
          Magento_Catalog/ - 0
          Magento_Theme/ - 0
          composer.json - 467
          etc/ - 0
          i18n/ - 0
          media/ - 0
          registration.php - 173
          theme.xml - 312
          web/ - 0
DEBUG - "packt-bookstore-bookstore.1.0.0.zip": Top level directory - <>.
DEBUG - "packt-bookstore-bookstore.1.0.0.zip": composer.json
          {
              "name": "packt/bookstore",
              "description": "BookStore theme",
              "require": {
                  "php": "~5.5.0|~5.6.0|~7.0.0",
                  "magento/theme-frontend-luma": "~100.0",
                  "magento/framework": "~100.0"
              },
              "type": "magento2-theme",
              "version": "1.0.0",
              "license": [
                  "OSL-3.0",
                  "AFL-3.0"
              ],
              "autoload": {
                  "files": [ "registration.php" ],
                  "psr-4": {
                      "Packt\\BookStore\\": ""
                  }
              }
          }
DEBUG - "packt-bookstore-bookstore.1.0.0.zip": Success, passed all the validation checks.
```

Hosting your theme

You can share your Magento theme and host your code on different services to achieve greater interaction with your team or even with the Magento development community. Remember that the standard control system software version used by the Magento development community is Git.

There are some options frequently used in the market, so you can distribute your code and share your work. Let's look at some of these options.

Hosting your project on GitHub and Packagist

The most common method of hosting your code/theme is to use GitHub. Once you have created a repository, you can get help from the Magento developer community if you are working on an open source project or even one for learning purposes.

The major point of using GitHub is the question of your portfolio and the publication of your Magento 2 projects developed, which certainly will make a difference when you are looking for employment opportunities and trying to get selected for new projects.

GitHub has a specific help area for users that provides a collection of documentation that developers may find useful. GitHub Help can be accessed directly at `https://help.github.com/`:

To create a GitHub repository, you can consult the official documentation, available at `https://help.github.com/articles/create-a-repo/`.

Once you have your project published on GitHub, you can use the **Packagist** (`https://pac kagist.org/`) service by creating a new account and entering the link of your GitHub package on Packagist:

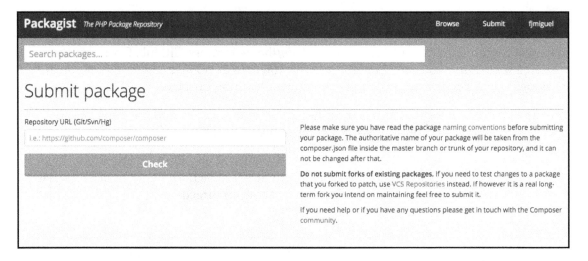

Packagist collects information automatically from the available `composer.json` file in the GitHub repository, creating your reference to use in other projects.

Hosting your project in a private repository

In some cases, you will be developing your project for private clients and companies. In case you want to keep your version control in private mode, you can use the following procedure:

1. Create your own package composer repository using the **Toran** service (`https:/ /toranproxy.com/`).
2. Create your package as previously described.
3. Send your package to your private repository.
4. Add the following to your `composer.json` file:

```
{
    "repositories": [
        {
            "type": "composer",
            "url": [repository url here]
        }
    ]
```

```
}
```

Magento Marketplace

According to Magento, Marketplace (`https://marketplace.magento.com/`) is the largest global e-commerce resource for applications and services that extend Magento solutions with powerful new features and functionality.

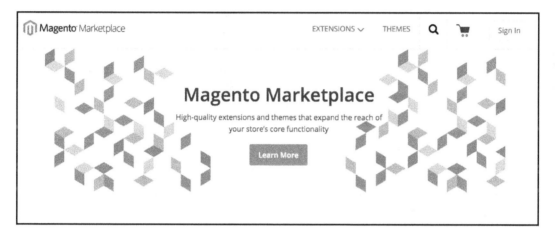

Once you have finished developing the first version of your theme, you can upload your project to be a part of the official marketplace of Magento. In addition to allowing theme uploads, Magento Marketplace also allows you to upload **shared packages** and **extensions** (modules).

To learn more about shared packages, visit `http://docs.magento.com/ma rketplace/user_guide/extensions/shared-package-submit.html`.

Submitting your theme

After the compression and validation processes, you can send your project to be distributed via Magento Marketplace.

For this, you should confirm an account on the **developer portal** (`https://developer.mage nto.com/customer/account/`) with a valid e-mail and personal information about the scope of your activities.

After this confirmation, you will have access to the extensions area at `https://developer.magento.com/extension/extension/list/`, where you will find options to submit themes and extensions:

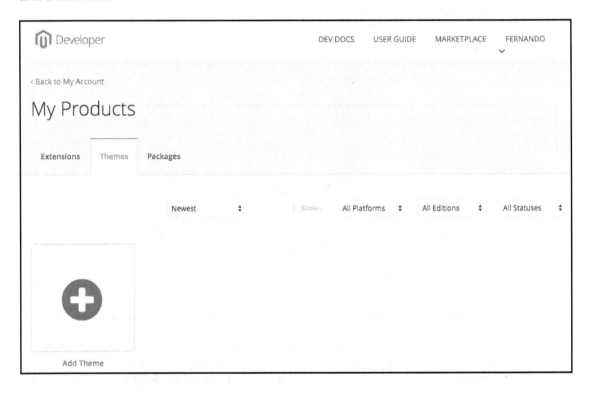

After clicking on the **Add Theme** button, you will need to answer a questionnaire:

- Which Magento platform your theme will work on
- The name of your theme
- Whether your theme will have additional services
- Additional functionalities your theme has
- What makes your theme unique

Tell us about this theme

What platform is your theme compatible with?

Magento 1.x	Magento 2.x

What's the title of your theme

Does your theme offer any additional services beyond the theme code itself?
This could include SAAS connections, recurring subscriptions, upgrades or paid support services provided either through you or a third party.

Yes, my theme offers additional services	No, my theme does not offer additional services

Is this theme already on Magento Connect ?
Magento Connect is our previous extension and theme store and hosts Magento 2.x products only.

Yes, it is   No, it is not

After the questionnaire, you will need to fill in the details of your extension, as follows:

- Extension title
- Public version
- Package file (upload)

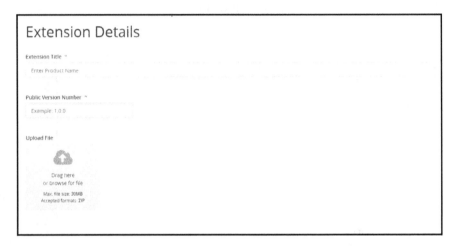

The submitted theme will be evaluated by a technical review, and you will be able to see the evaluation progress through your e-mail and the control panel of the Magento developer area.

You can find more information about Magento Marketplace at the following link:`http://docs.magento.com/marketplace/user_guide/getting-started.html`

Summary

In this chapter, you learned about the theme packaging process besides validation according to the minimum requirements for its publication on Magento Marketplace.

You are now ready to develop your solutions! There is still a lot of work left, but I encourage you to seek your way as a Magento theme developer by putting a lot of study, research, and application into the area. Participate in events, be collaborative and count on the community's support.

Good luck and success in your career path!

Index